W9-BRU-388

Egypt

Egypt

Revised Edition

BY ANN HEINRICHS

*Enchantment of the World
Second Series*

Children's Press®

A Division of Scholastic Inc.

NEW YORK   TORONTO   LONDON   AUCKLAND   SYDNEY
MEXICO CITY   NEW DELHI   HONG KONG
DANBURY, CONNECTICUT

Frontispiece: Market in Cairo

Consultant: Dr. Peter Sluglett, Professor of Middle Eastern History, University of Utah, Salt Lake City

Please note: All statistics are as up-to-date as possible at the time of publication.

Book production by Herman Adler Design

Library of Congress Cataloging-in-Publication Data

Heinrichs, Ann.
  Egypt, revised edition / by Ann Heinrichs—Rev. ed.
    p. cm. — (Enchantment of the world. Second series)
  Includes index.
  ISBN-10: 0-516-24866-9
  ISBN-13: 978-0-516-24866-0
  1. Egypt—Juvenile literature. I. Title. II. Series.
  DT49.H45 2007
  962—dc22   2005028214

CHILDREN'S PRESS and associated logos are trademarks and/or registered
trademarks of Scholastic Library Publishing. SCHOLASTIC and associated logos
are trademarks and/or registered trademarks of Scholastic Inc.
1 2 3 4 5 6 7 8 9 10 R 16 15 14 13 12 11 10 09 08 07

Egypt

Cover photo:
Temple of
Abu Simbel

Contents

CHAPTER

ONE "Things of Unspeakable Greatness"................... 8

TWO Black Land, Red Land............................. 14

THREE Desert Life.................................... 28

FOUR Land of the Pharaohs.......................... 38

FIVE Governing Egypt................................. 64

SIX Fruits of Their Labor 74

SEVEN Crowded Cities, Common Bonds 86

EIGHT People of God 94

NINE Life and Learning............................. 104

TEN The Many Flavors of Life 118

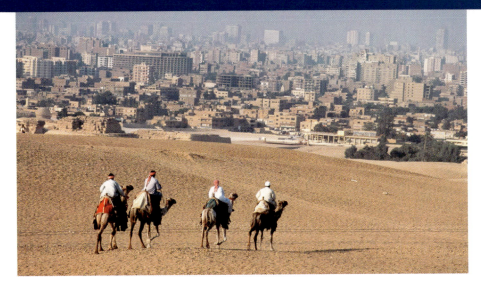
Camels near Cairo

Timeline **128**

Fast Facts **130**

To Find Out More **134**

Index **136**

Statue of a scribe

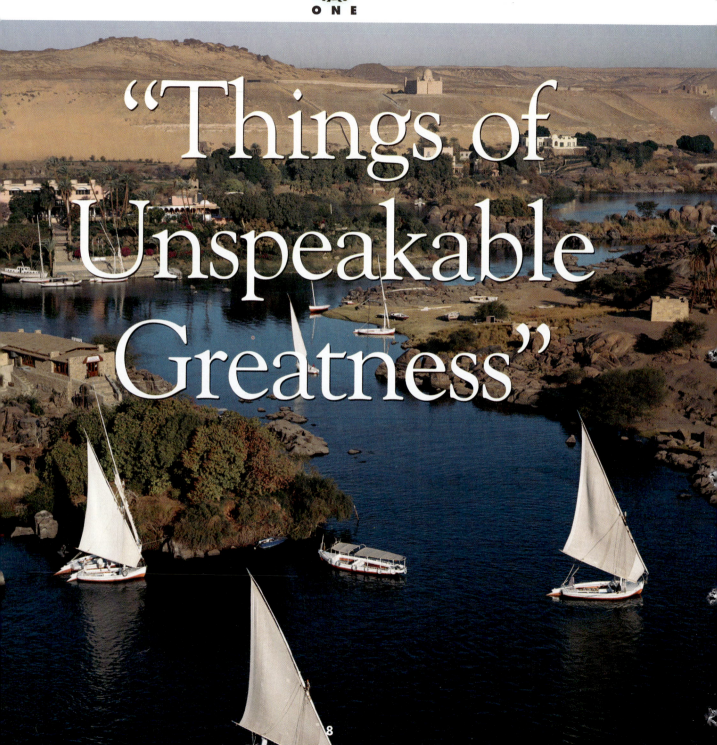

CHAPTER ONE

"Things of Unspeakable Greatness"

R AWIA WOKE EARLY THAT MORNING. THE FIRST RAYS OF sun were just peeping over the hills. She did not know what the day would bring, but she was excited. Today was the first day of school!

Opening day at school does not seem unusual, but it was for Rawia. Her little farming community in Egypt had just built its first schoolhouse. No one in her family had ever attended school. And many people believed girls did not need an education. Some villagers wondered, "What does a girl need to study for?" Others complained that they needed the children to work in the fields.

Opposite: **Boats travel the Nile near Aswan**

Young girls picking cotton. Egypt produces about 250,000 tons of cotton each year.

Rawia's parents agreed to send her to school, though. Soon she was reading, writing, and working math problems. Her father, a shopkeeper, quickly grew to appreciate her new skills.

"Until Rawia went to school, my store accounts were in a complete mess," he said. "But before long, she was taking care of all the books for me, as well as helping her elder sister to read and write."

Other schoolchildren in Rawia's village made a difference in their families, too. They could read the labels on medicine bottles. They could read instructions on sacks of fertilizer for the crops. Villagers began to realize that education was a great benefit—for girls as well as boys.

A teacher and students in a rural school. It is estimated that 82 percent of Egyptian girls attend elementary school.

Now, eight years later, Rawia and others like her have a chance to fulfill their dreams of going to college. "Many of the people [in my village] want me to become a doctor," says one girl. "I myself want to be a teacher, so that I can pass on some of what I've learned to other children."

Rawia's experience is typical of the changes Egypt is undergoing today. Like Rawia's village, the country lives with one foot in the past and the other foot in the future. Most farmers

EGYPT

- ● Cities of over 200,000 people
- ○ Other cities
- ✪ National capital
- ∴ Archaeological site

0   150 miles

0   150 kilometers

Mediterranean Sea

SYRIA

ISRAEL   West Bank

Gaza Strip

JORDAN

As-Sallum   Matruh   Rosetta   El Mahalla   Port Said
Ra's al-Hikmah   El Kubra   Al Arish
Alexandria   Damanhur   El Mansura
Sidi 'Abd ar-Rahman   Tanta   Zagazig   Ismailia
Shoubra al-Kheima   *Suez Canal*
Qarah   Giza   Cairo   Suez
Siwa   Pyramids of Giza   As-Saff   An-Nakhl
Az-Zaytun   Fayyum   Nasir
Abu Zanimah
Biba   Beni Suef
Gulf of Suez   *Gulf of Aqaba*
Mandishah   Beni Mazar   Maghaghah
Samalut   El Minya   Ra's   Sharm
Mallawi   Gharib   el-Sheikh
Dayrut   Abnub   Jamsah
Ras Muhammad National Park
Asyut   Timq   Hurghada
Sawhaj   Jirja
Qena
Al Qasr   Balat   Qift
Kharga   Valley of the Kings   Thebes   Al Qusayr
Mut   Tunaydah   Luxor
Bulaq   Isna   Idfu   Marsa al-Alam
Baris   Iqlit
Daraw
Aswan
Aswan High Dam   Mina Baranis
Lake Nasser
Abu Simbel   Halaib Triangle

LIBYA

Nile R.

SAUDI ARABIA

Red Sea

SUDAN

use centuries-old methods. They expect their children to help out with the farmwork. School would take them away from their duties. It's a tradition, too, that girls work in the home and marry in their early teens.

Vendors sell vegetables in a market.

Egypt's government, however, is challenging many old ways. In the 1990s, the government teamed up with international organizations to build schools in rural areas. Now, several thousand new schools dot the countryside. Education for girls is a major part of this new thrust.

Not everyone is sure these changes are good. Most Egyptians are Muslims, and their religion of Islam affects many activities of daily life. The strictest Muslims believe women and girls belong in the home. School and a career would upset the good of society.

Despite their disagreements, however, Egyptians are more alike than they are different. Arab culture permeates their everyday lives. They share the Arabic language, music, art, festivals, and food. In their religion, too, Egyptians find a sense of community that runs deeper than their differences.

Egyptians also share a pride in their ancient heritage. Almost 2,500 years ago, the Greek historian Herodotus visited Egypt. He was astonished by what he saw. "Nowhere are there so many marvelous things," he wrote, "nor in the whole world are there to be seen so many things of unspeakable greatness."

Ancient Egyptians developed one of the earliest civilizations on earth. How did they build their fabulous pyramids, temples, and tombs? We may never know.

In Egypt's Valley of the Kings, a laborer digs out a newly discovered tomb. It is a dirty, backbreaking job in the sweltering desert sun. When a visitor asks how he feels about his task, the young man smiles proudly.

"I am descended from the people who built this tomb," he replies. "I can feel their blood is in me."

Laborers dig out a tomb in the Valley of the Kings. The valley contains the tombs of sixty-four pharaohs and other ancient Egyptian nobles.

Black Land, Red Land

E GYPT IS A DESERT WITH A RIVER RUNNING THROUGH IT. About 96 percent of Egypt's land is desert. But the life-giving Nile, the longest river in the world, flows between its Western and Eastern deserts. Ancient Egyptians called their land *Kemet*, meaning "black land," for the rich soil of the Nile River valley. *Deshret*, the "red land," was the surrounding desert.

Egypt covers an area almost as large as the states of Texas and New Mexico combined. It is slightly larger than the Canadian province of British Columbia. People often talk about Upper Egypt and Lower Egypt. But they're the opposite of how they appear on a map. Upper Egypt and the Upper Nile are in the south, where the land is higher. Lower Egypt and the Lower Nile are in the north.

Opposite: **Camel riders approach Cairo from the desert.**

Women carry baskets along the Nile River.

Nearly all of Egypt is in the continent of Africa. The Sinai Peninsula is the only part of Egypt that lies in Asia. It makes up Egypt's northeast corner, beyond the Suez Canal. The canal marks the dividing line between the two continents.

The Deserts

Egypt's two largest land regions are the Western Desert and the Eastern Desert. The Western Desert, also called the Libyan Desert, covers about two-thirds of the country. It is part of North Africa's great Sahara Desert, extending west into Libya and south into Sudan.

The White Desert is part of the greater Western Desert. The white comes from the chalk rock that has been ground into dust.

Egypt's Geographic Features

Area: 386,900 square miles (1,002,071 sq km)

Borders: The Mediterranean Sea to the north; the Gaza Strip, Israel, and the Red Sea to the east; Sudan to the south; and Libya to the west

Highest Elevation: Jabal Katrina (Mount Saint Catherine), 8,652 feet (2,637 m)

Lowest Elevation: In the Qattara Depression, 436 feet (133 m) below sea level

Length of Coastlines: About 620 miles (1,000 km) on the Mediterranean Sea; about 1,200 miles (1,900 km) on the Red Sea and the Gulf of Aqaba

Greatest Distance, North to South: 675 miles (1,086 km)

Greatest Distance, East to West: 780 miles (1,255 km)

Longest River: The Nile, the world's longest river, about 750 miles (1,200 km) long in Egypt and about 4,160 miles (6,695 km) in total

Largest Lake: Lake Nasser (the world's second-largest artificial lake)

Largest Desert: The Western Desert (about two-thirds of Egypt's land area)

Average Annual Rainfall: Alexandria, 7 inches (18 cm); Aswan, 0.1 inch (.25 cm)

Average Temperatures: Alexandria, 59°F (15°C) in January, 79°F (26°C) in July; Aswan, 62°F (17°C) in January, 93°F (34°C) in July

The Western Desert is a vast expanse of rippling sand, blown by ever-shifting winds. Rocky ridges jut out here and there. In some places, the sand piles up to form graceful dunes.

The warm waters of the Red Sea coast at Hurghada have become a popular tourist destination.

The desert sands can be destructive, however, when they blow over farms and villages. The Qattara Depression, a sunken area in the north, contains Egypt's lowest point.

The Eastern Desert is also called the Arabian Desert. Long ago, before the Red Sea existed, the Eastern Desert was joined to the Arabian Peninsula. From the east bank of the Nile, the Eastern Desert slopes gently upward into rocky hills that line the seacoast. Deep ravines called *wadis* cut through the hills.

Few people live in the Eastern Desert, but several small towns lie along the coast. Hurghada is the center for activities related to Egypt's oil drilling in the Red Sea. The northern coastal waters near Hurghada are severely polluted. South of the town, though, the water is clean enough to attract divers who explore the coast's spectacular coral reefs.

The Nile Valley and Delta

Without the Nile River, Egypt would be one huge desert. But the Nile has nourished Egypt's farms for thousands of years.

The waters of the Nile flow from two sources. The White Nile, the longer branch, rises in Burundi, deep in the heart of Africa. From there to the Mediterranean Sea, the Nile is about 4,160 miles (6,695 kilometers) long. Most of the Nile's water, however, comes from the Blue Nile, which rises in the highlands of Ethiopia. The torrential summer rains there are the same ones that cause annual floods in Egypt. These two branches, the White Nile and the Blue Nile, join in central Sudan to form one river, which flows into Egypt.

Near Cairo, Egypt's capital city, the Nile fans out into dozens of streams that empty into the Mediterranean. This sediment-rich area is named the Delta, after the Greek letter shaped like a triangle (Δ). The Delta stretches about 100 miles (160 km)

The floodplain of the Nile River provides rich soil good for growing crops such as rice.

Looking at Egypt's Cities

Alexandria (right) was founded by Alexander the Great in 332 B.C, after his Greek armies took over Egypt. As a center of science and learning, Alexandria became one of the greatest cities of the ancient world. The Library of Alexandria was the most famous library of ancient times.

Today, Alexandria is Egypt's second-largest city and a busy port on the Mediterranean Sea. Many sites recall the city's glorious past. The Greco-Roman Museum preserves objects from Alexandria's old period. The Bibliotheca Alexandrina, opened in 2002, was built to commemorate Alexandria's ancient library. Two obelisks, or tall stone towers, called Cleopatra's Needles stand near the waterfront. Archaeologists are still exploring Alexandria's offshore waters in search of ancient treasures. They have already found ruins of the Pharos, a lighthouse that is considered one of the Seven Wonders of the Ancient World.

Giza, Egypt's third-largest city, is a suburb of Cairo, Egypt's largest city. Lying on the west bank of the Nile, it is the site of some of Egypt's most famous monuments—three towering pyramids and the Sphinx. Today, Giza is home to the University of Cairo, the Academy of the Arabic Language, and many museums, embassies, and government offices. It is also the center of Egypt's motion-picture industry and has a busy entertainment district.

Luxor is one of Egypt's oldest cities. It stands on the east bank of the Nile, on the site of Upper Egypt's ancient capital city of Thebes. Pharaoh Amenhotep III built the Temple of Luxor in the 1300s B.C. Ramses II added giant statues of himself in the temple's court.

The Avenue of the Sphinxes connects the Luxor temple to the Temple of Amun at nearby Karnak. Across the Nile from Luxor is the necropolis, or city of the dead. This ancient cemetery includes the tomb sites known as the Valley of the Kings and the Valley of the Queens.

Shoubra al-Kheima is a northern suburb of Cairo. Located on the Nile's east bank, it was once a market center for farm products from the Nile Delta, and Egypt's first European-style schools and factories were built there in the 1820s. Today, it is an industrial center specializing in textiles, glass, and ceramics.

Port Said is one of Egypt's major ports. It lies on the Mediterranean Sea at the northern end of the Suez Canal. Port Said was founded in the 1860s while the canal was being built. Suez is a port city at the southern end of the Suez Canal, at the head of the Gulf of Suez.

from north to south and about 160 miles (260 km) along the coast. Almost all of Egypt's farmland is in the Delta and in the narrow strip along the river. Most of Egypt's people live in these areas, too. The historic city of Alexandria sits right on the seacoast.

Western Desert Oases

An oasis is an area in the desert where underground water flows. In Egypt's Western Desert oases, the water gushes up in springs and gathers into ponds and wells surrounded by tall date palms and lush gardens. In some oases, the underground waters feed rich, green valleys.

Underground waters allow crops to be grown at Farafra oasis.

The oases closest to the Nile—Bahariya, Farafra, Dakhla, and Kharga—are called the New Valley oases. Long ago, a branch of the Nile flowed through them. Other western oases are Baris, south of Kharga, and Siwa, near the Libyan border.

A large settlement called the Fayyum lies just west of the Nile. Its palm trees, mountains, and ancient ruins are surrounded by desert. But the Fayyum is not really an oasis. Its water supply comes from a branch of the Nile.

Oasis water, rich with sulfur and other minerals, is known for its health benefits. People come from all over the world to bathe in these waters. The silt—bits of sediment that sink to the bottom—is also used to treat bone, skin, muscle, and stomach problems.

A canal connecting to the Nile allows trees to thrive in the Fayyum. It is a rich argricultural region where grains, cotton, grapes and many other products are grown.

Ten thousand people had to move because their homes were flooded when Lake Nasser was formed.

Lake Nasser and the Aswan High Dam

Lake Nasser, south of Aswan, is Egypt's largest lake. It stretches for 312 miles (502 km) across Egypt's border into Sudan. Lake Nasser is an artificial lake. It was created in the 1960s by building the Aswan High Dam across the Nile.

In the 1950s, President Gamal Abdel Nasser decided to build the Aswan High Dam. Waters building up behind the dam would form a lake, but that presented a problem. The lake would flood ancient monuments such as the Temples of Abu Simbel and Philae. Thousands of engineers and laborers from all over the world formed a "rescue team" to save the monuments. Stone by stone, they were moved to higher ground. This massive project took more than ten years. The Aswan High Dam and its power station began operating in 1968.

An irrigation system channels water in Dakhla oasis.

Damming the Nile has brought many benefits. It controls Egypt's annual floodwaters, enabling farmers to grow crops year-round, and it makes irrigation easier. Also, water rushing over the dam produces hydroelectric power and improves boat travel on the Nile.

The dam has its drawbacks, though. Silt from the river gets trapped in Lake Nasser, so the Nile Valley no longer gets that natural fertilizer. The Delta has suffered, too. Without the Nile's natural gushing force, salt water from the Mediterranean creeps upstream. This higher salt content makes the land less fertile. And without steady silt deposits, the Mediterranean coast is eroding, or washing away.

The Sinai Peninsula

The Sinai Peninsula is part desert and part rocky mountains. It has more camel trails than roads. Bedouin nomads (wanderers) have lived in the Sinai for centuries. Now, vacationers and tourists visit the Sinai's seaside resort towns.

Rocky mountain ranges rise in the south. The best-known peaks are Jabal Katrina (Mount Saint Catherine)—Egypt's highest point—and Jabal Musa (Mount Sinai). The Colored Canyon, not far from Mount Sinai, has striped rock formations in shades of pink, orange, and yellow.

Goats graze near Mount Sinai.

Southern Sinai is flanked by two arms of the Red Sea—the Gulf of Suez on the west and the Gulf of Aqaba on the east. Tourists enjoy south Sinai's coastal resort cities. Some are simple towns with thatched-roof waterfront huts, while others offer lavish hotels, restaurants, and entertainment. Snorkeling and scuba diving are major attractions. The resort city of Sharm el-Sheikh, on the peninsula's southern tip, was once a small fishing village. Now it's the Sinai's largest city.

Vacationers flock to the Red Sea resort city of Sharm el-Sheikh.

Climate

Egypt has two seasons—summer and winter. Summers, from May through October, are sweltering. In July, the average high in Aswan is 106°F (41°C). To escape the heat, many Egyptians head for the cool sea breezes of the Mediterranean coast. Winters—November through April—are mild and sometimes cool. All year long, temperatures in Upper Egypt are higher than those in the north. Mountainous regions of the Sinai can be quite chilly.

A Bedouin man with camels in the mountains of the Sinai

In the desert, the glaring sun makes midday trips dangerous. Travelers on camels often sleep during the hottest part of the day. They venture out before mid-morning and after sundown. Nights in the desert can be icy cold, though, because sand does not retain the sun's heat. In April, desert dwellers take cover during the *khamsin*—a hot, dry wind from the south that causes blinding sandstorms.

Most of Egypt's rain falls in the winter near the Mediterranean. It almost never rains in the desert. Snow is seen only on the Sinai's highest mountaintops, where around 11 inches (28 centimeters) fall every year.

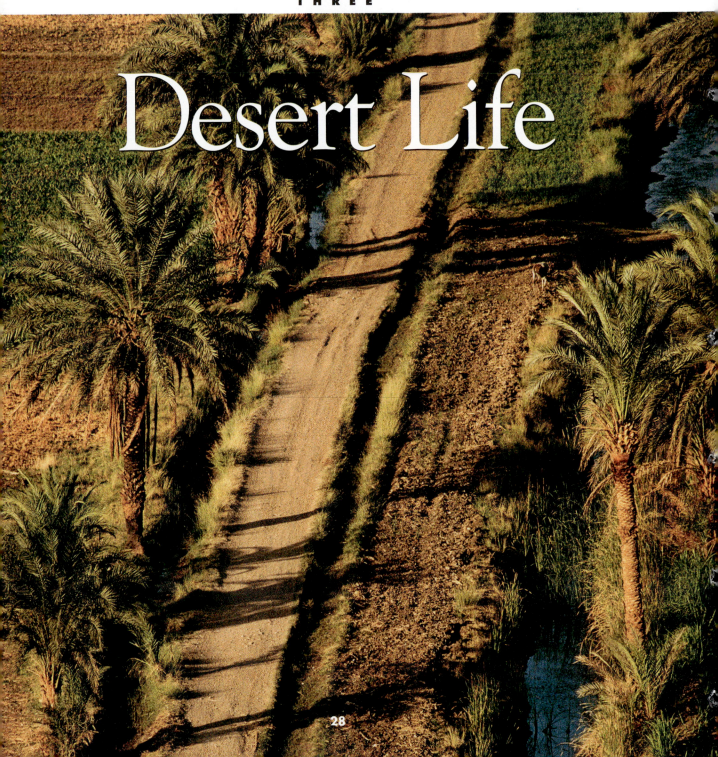

Desert Life

Hundreds of years ago, the Nile River Valley was teeming with wildlife. Lions emerged from the riverside thickets to drink at the water's edge. Hippopotamuses submerged themselves in the cool waters. The lions and hippos are gone now, but the Nile Valley still teems with wildlife. One of the most fearsome river creatures is the Nile crocodile. These meat eaters have powerful jaws, and the crocodiles sometimes work together to take down much larger animals.

Egypt's temples and pyramids make safe homes for many animals. The monuments shelter them from the desert heat and provide good hiding places. Inside, colonies of bats cling to the ceilings and walls. The golden spiny mouse sleeps in a dark

Opposite: **Fields and a country road near Luxor in the Nile River Valley**

The golden spiny mouse thrives in dry, rocky regions. It's golden brown color helps it blend in with the landscape.

corner in the daytime and comes out at night. The orange head of the agama, or gray lizard, blends in with the stones.

With its sweltering days and chilly nights, the desert is a rough habitat for animals. Skinks, lizards, and other reptiles can stand these extremes, but some animals, such as hyenas and mice, creep out only at night.

Furry little fennecs are foxes that weigh only about 3 pounds (1.4 kilograms). They're also called desert foxes or sand foxes. Fennecs spend the day in their underground burrows to escape the heat. They come out at night to feed on insects, fruit, and small animals. Their big eyes and long ears help them locate prey—and predators.

A fennec fox has huge ears. Body heat escapes through its big ears, cooling the fox down.

The deserts are also home to plenty of snakes. The venomous saw-scaled viper is a relative of the rattlesnake. Its scales make a scratchy sound as it moves across the sand. Sand boas, however, are not dangerous to humans. They help keep down the rodent population and are a protected species.

The ibex, a wild mountain goat with long, curved horns, scampers over steep, rocky slopes in the Sinai. In the daytime, a Sinai rodent called the rock hyrax basks in the sun. At night, it eats acacia plants.

The horns of an ibex can reach 3 feet (1 meter) long.

More Than a Pet

Cats were sacred animals in ancient Egypt. They were thought to represent the goddess Bastet, daughter of the sun god Re. Bronze statues of cats filled Bastet's temple near Zagazig. Cats were mummified and buried in special cat cemeteries. Hundreds of thousands of cats were found in a cemetery in Thebes.

Wild Cats

It was in Egypt that cats were first tamed. People keep cats as pets in Egypt today, but many kinds of wild cats still roam the deserts, and wild swamp cats slink around in the Delta.

The Kaffir cat is also called the Egyptian wild cat. Its coloring is just like a tabby cat's. The main difference is that its tail is shorter and thicker. It hunts rodents, birds, and snakes, just as domestic cats do.

Sand cats, which are about the size of housecats, are built for desert living. Their paws have thick fur on the bottom to protect their feet from the burning sands. Sand cats can go for long periods without drinking water. They hunt small rodents, and they get fluids from the bodies of their prey.

Caracals, or desert lynx, are Egypt's largest wild cats. Their golden-brown color blends in with the desert sands. Tufts of black hair stick up on the top of their long, pointy ears. Caracals are swift runners. This allows them to pounce on birds, their main prey.

Ships of the Desert

People have used camels to travel through the desert for thousands of years. Camels can be seen everywhere in Egypt, from desert wastelands to city streets. They're called "ships of the desert" because they navigate vast oceans of sand. A camel can carry a 500-pound (270 kg) load for 30 miles (48 km). Camels bred for racing can run up to 10 miles (16 km) per hour for eighteen hours. These hardy beasts can travel for weeks without eating food or drinking water. When they have a chance to drink water, they fill up. A camel can drink 25 gallons (95 liters) of water without stopping. Camels have a bad reputation for spitting, kicking, and biting, but their gentle, lurching pace is a first-class comfort on long trips.

Birds

Many birds live near the Nile and feed on fish. The pied kingfisher dives in and snaps up fish with its long bill. Long-legged herons also wade and fish along the Nile. Huge flocks of flamingos swoop down upon the Nile in the winter. Their pink color comes from the food they eat. The flamingos' white feathers take on a pink color when the birds eat tiny pink brine shrimp!

A heron perches on a wire near Aswan.

The Beetle That Pushed the Sun

The scarab is a beetle that crawls along pushing a huge ball of dung, or animal waste. To ancient Egyptians, the scarab represented Khepri, the god of the dawning sun. All through the night, Khepri pushed the sun across the darkness so that it could rise the next day. Good-luck charms, jewelry, and signature seals are still made in the shape of scarabs.

Many kinds of ibis live near the Nile. They have powerful legs for wading in the water and long, curved bills for snatching fish. The ibis has been around since ancient times. It was a symbol of the god Thoth, who was usually pictured with the head of an ibis.

An egret takes flight in a wildlife haven at Wadi al Rayan.

Gulls, ospreys, and spoonbills nest on the Red Sea coast. Lake Nasser is a haven for migrating birds. Pelicans, geese, terns, plovers, and warblers are seen along the shore. Cattle egrets are a common sight in farming areas. They dip over the fields looking for insects and frogs. Doves, bee-eaters, and black kites live in both the countryside and the city. Hoopoes are city birds that cruise grassy patches for insects. Rock martins and white-crowned wheatears build their nests in rocky nooks and crevices.

St. John's Reef is one of the top diving spots in the Red Sea. It is famed for its large variety of fish.

Life in the Coral Reefs

Coral reefs line the underwater banks of the Red Sea. A coral reef is actually made of skeletons. Tiny animals called coral polyps live in huge colonies along the coast. When the polyps die, new polyps attach themselves to the skeletons. Generation after generation, millions of skeletons build up to form a massive reef.

The coral reef is home to a rainbow of amazing sea creatures—red sponges, green sea anemones, prickly sea urchins, and feathery fan worms. In and out of this maze swim blue tangs, groupers, angelfish, butterfly fish, lionfish, surgeonfish, sharks, and moray eels. Inching along the bottom are sea slugs and giant clams.

Ras Muhammad National Park

Egypt has more than twenty national parks and nature preserves. The oldest is Ras Muhammad National Park, on the southern tip of the Sinai Peninsula. This park protects the animals and plants of its deserts, mangrove forests, and nearby waters. Dorcas gazelles, Nubian ibex, and foxes roam the park. Dozens of bird species nest there. Other birds, such as white storks, pass through on their migrations. Green turtles and hawksbill turtles, both threatened species, often come ashore. Offshore are spectacular coral reefs. Divers can see manta rays, reef sharks, parrot fish, lionfish, and 6-foot (1.8 m) Napoleon fish. Part of the waters are an eel garden. Some of its eels grow as long as 66 feet (20 m).

Plants

In Egypt, most plant life hugs the Nile. As early as 3500 B.C., Egyptians used fibers of the papyrus plant to make writing paper. Today, papyrus is grown mainly in the Delta region and rarely grows in the wild. The lotus, a flowering water plant that once grew all along the Nile, was the royal symbol for Upper Egypt. Today, it is found only in the Delta, in hidden bends of the Nile, and in the Fayyum. Tall reeds thrive along the Nile's banks and on its islands. Acacias brighten the riverbanks with their yellow flowers. The water hyacinth is a beautiful, blue-flowered pest. This hardy plant spreads fast and clogs irrigation canals.

Date palms grow along the Nile and in the oases along with groves of citrus, pomegranate, and apricot trees. A sharp, aromatic smell is a sign that eucalyptus trees are nearby. Egypt's only forests are the mangrove forests on the coasts of the Red Sea and the southeast Sinai. The roots of saltwater mangrove trees grow partly underwater and partly above the surface.

Egyptians have been growing date palms along the Nile River for thousands of years.

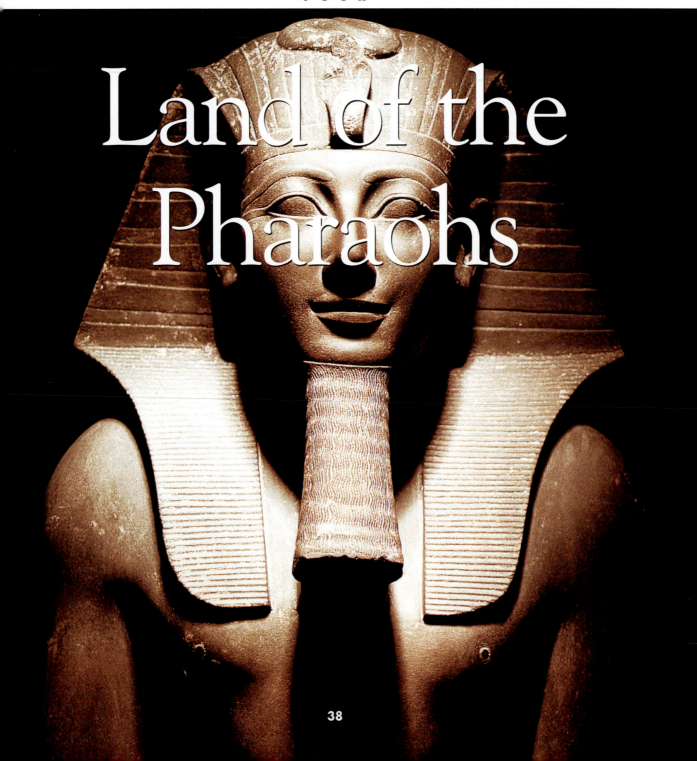

Land of the Pharaohs

P EOPLE WERE FARMING ALONG THE NILE AS EARLY AS 5000 B.C. Over time, the people along the Nile settled into two kingdoms—Upper Egypt in the south, and Lower Egypt in the Delta. In about 3100 B.C., Menes, a king of Upper Egypt, united the two kingdoms. Menes was honored as Egypt's first pharaoh, or king. Pharaohs kept their power in the family. Ancient Egypt was governed by one dynasty, or ruling family, after another. Thirty dynasties of pharaohs reigned in Egypt between 3100 B.C. and 332 B.C.

Opposite: **A statue of Thutmose III from Egypt's Eighteenth Dynasty, around 1450 B.C.**

An ancient statue of a scribe found in a tomb at Giza

Ancient Egyptian Society

The pharaoh and his family were at the top rung of Egyptian society. They lived in great luxury. Alabaster lamps, golden beds and chairs, and exotic woods inlaid with ivory decorated their homes. Servants took care of their every need. Musicians and dancers amused guests at their lavish banquets. Other members of the upper class were priests, nobles, doctors, and high-ranking army officers.

Artisans, merchants, and engineers made up the middle class. Scribes, or professional writers, held a special place of honor. Every family hoped to have a son who would become a scribe. The scribes wrote letters and government documents and recorded the pharaohs' decrees.

The common people were farmers, laborers, and soldiers. Farming took only part of the year, so many farmers spent several months working on the pharaohs' construction projects.

Dressing in Ancient Egypt

Makeup and jewelry were important in ancient Egypt. Makeup was made from minerals and plants. Gypsum was mixed with soot to make a sparkly eye shadow. Both men and women wore a black sooty substance called kohl as an eyeliner. Women also painted their fingernails and colored their lips red. Hair ornaments were common. Upper-class women wore earrings, bracelets, armbands, and necklaces of gold and precious stones.

Both men and women wore lightweight linen skirts or robes. Lower-class people went barefoot, while the upper classes wore leather sandals. Shoulder-length head coverings protected workers from the heat of the sun. Upper-class men and women wore wigs. On festive evenings, women sometimes wore a cone of perfumed animal fat on their heads. As the night wore on, the fat melted, drenching them with sweet-smelling oil.

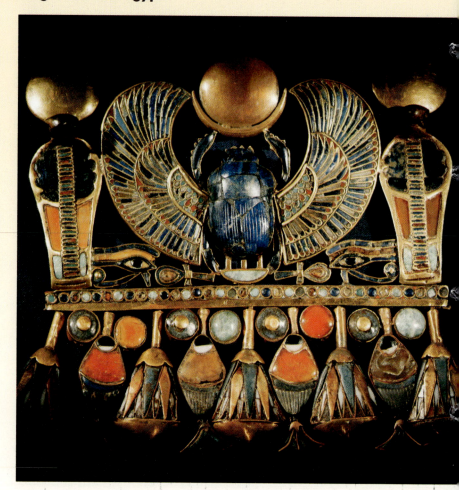

Women in ancient Egypt had more rights than women in many cultures have today. They could own property, buy and sell goods, and inherit wealth. Wives could even sue for divorce if they had a good reason.

An ointment jar from 1550–1295 B.C.

The Cycle of Floods

Ancient Egyptians divided the year into three seasons of four months each. The new year began with the flooding of the Nile in July. In November, as the waters receded, the plowing and planting season began. The dry season lasted from March to July. Then crops were harvested and stored before the rains came again.

The floodwaters left behind silt that fertilized the fields and produced abundant crops. Mud along the riverbank was made into pots, jars, tiles, and other ceramics. People measured the rise and fall of the Nile's water level with a nilometer—a series of marks on riverside rocks or cliffs.

Farmers produced more than enough food for Egypt's people. The pharaohs' storehouses brimmed over with the food they collected as taxes. Grain and other crops were traded with neighboring peoples in Africa and Asia.

Hieroglyphs

Egyptians were writing with picture symbols called hieroglyphs as early as 3000 B.C. Some symbols stood for sounds. Others showed whether a word was singular or plural, or a noun or a verb. By 300 B.C., the Egyptian alphabet consisted of more than seven hundred hieroglyphic symbols.

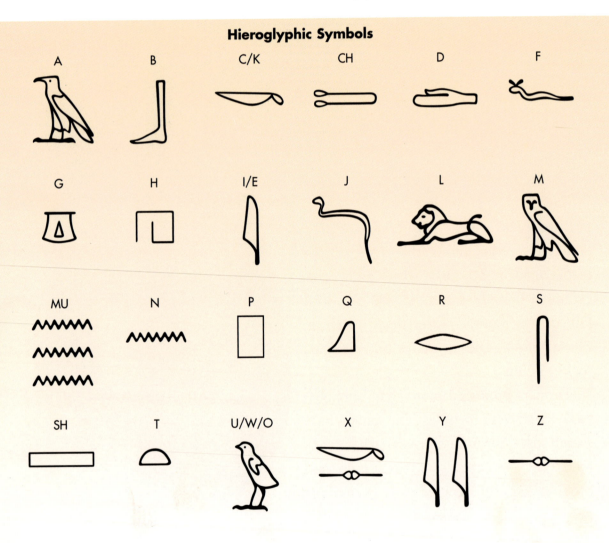

Hieroglyphic Symbols

Gods and Goddesses

Ancient Egyptians worshipped many gods and goddesses. They believed their gods caused the sun to rise, the Nile to flood, the crops to grow, and the cows to give milk. Each town and family had its own special gods. The pharaoh himself was seen as a god who protected the people.

Priests took care of the temples and made offerings at the proper times. Re, the sun god, was the most important of all Egyptian gods. Amun, the sun god of Thebes, was worshipped along with Re as a single deity, Amun-Re. His temple at Karnak, near Luxor, was a great center of worship for hundreds of years. One pharaoh after another built additions onto the temple, until it covered a huge area.

An ancient wall painting depicts the god Amun in one of his animal forms.

The age of 110 was believed to be the perfect life span, but it was more an ideal than a reality. Most people in those days did not live past their thirties. But every Egyptian, from pharaoh to laborer, believed in life after death. Given the proper burial rites, they could be immortal.

The Egyptians believed that the jackal-headed god Anubis escorted each soul into the afterlife. Osiris, god of the underworld, made a final judgment by the "weighing of the heart." A feather was put on one side of a scale, and the person's heart on the other side. If the heart was as light as the feather, the soul could enter eternity.

Egyptians also believed that the dead would enjoy all their earthly comforts in the afterlife. Burial chambers were filled with favorite possessions, clothes, furniture, games, and food. Even pet cats were preserved and buried with their masters.

Making Mummies

After death, the body was made into a mummy to keep it from decaying. This ensured a successful journey into the afterlife. Mummification could take as long as seventy days.

First, the body was packed in salt. This dried the tissues and kept them from breaking down. Then the internal organs were removed. Some were preserved in jars and buried with the body. Other organs were treated with herbs and put back into the body. The brain, believed to be worthless, was thrown away!

Embalming fluids and pastes were then applied to preserve the skin and the body's interior.

Finally, the body was wrapped round and round with white linen strips. Mummies of some pharaohs were encased in jewel-encrusted gold and placed in a stone coffin in the burial chamber. Scrolls of the *Book of the Dead* were buried with the body. This text was a sort of guidebook to the afterlife. It contained special prayers and instructions for getting through the mysterious world of the dead.

To make sure they would have eternal life, pharaohs built fabulous tombs for themselves. The earliest pharaohs built tombs called *mastabas*—low, flat-topped, mud-brick structures with slanting sides. Djoser, a pharaoh of the Third Dynasty, wanted a more glorious tomb, so his architect, Imhotep, built the first pyramid. It is called a step pyramid because its sides are like stair steps. Djoser's step pyramid still stands at Saqqara, near Memphis.

The Great Pyramid at Giza, just west of Cairo, was built around 2600 B.C. for the pharaoh Khufu. It was made of limestone blocks covered with sheer granite slabs that glistened in the sun. People could slide right down the sides. In later centuries, some of the granite was removed to make buildings in Cairo. Nearby are two other giant pyramids and the Great Sphinx, a massive stone lion with the head of a man.

It took more than 2,300,000 blocks of stone to build the Great Pyramid at Giza.

Who Is the Sphinx? Where Is Its Nose?

The Great Sphinx's head is six stories high, and its lion's body is four-fifths as long as a football field. Its face is believed to be a portrait of Khafre, son of Khufu. But some researchers think the statue was carved long before Khafre's time. They point to the rocks' erosion pattern, which looks more like water erosion than wind erosion. That would place the Sphinx in a time when heavy rains and floods were common in Egypt—perhaps up to ten thousand years ago. Regardless of its age, the Sphinx has been badly damaged by wind, sandstorms, rain, and pollution. Its nose is completely gone. Workers are now giving it a "face-lift" by restoring crumbling stones.

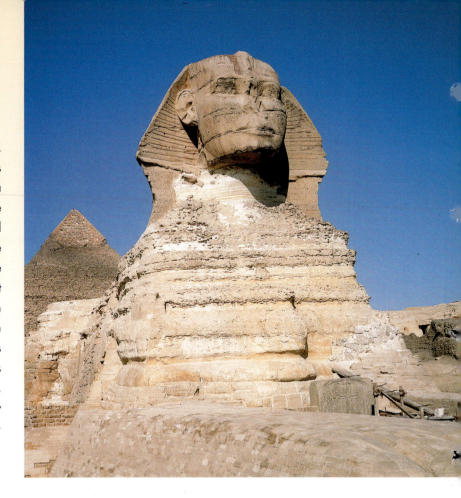

The ancient Egyptians left only a few clues about how they built the pyramids. From rock quarries at Aswan, stone blocks were floated down the Nile on rafts for 500 miles (800 km). Then the blocks were probably put on runners, like sleds, and hauled up wooden or stone ramps.

The Greek historian Herodotus says that one hundred thousand men worked on the Great Pyramid in three-month shifts. Then another one hundred thousand went to work. This went on for more than twenty years. How were the blocks lifted into place? According to Herodotus, they were lifted with a kind of crane that rested on lower-level stones.

Kingdoms Unite and Divide

The history of ancient Egypt may be divided into three major periods—the Old Kingdom, the Middle Kingdom, and the New Kingdom. Memphis, a few miles south of what is now Cairo, was Egypt's capital during the Old Kingdom period, beginning around 2575 B.C. Even in this early period, Egyptians were making paper from papyrus fibers and writing in hieroglyphs.

In time, the pharaohs' power weakened, and Egypt once again broke into separate districts. Mentuhotep II pulled the kingdom together in around 2040 B.C. He built his capital at Thebes, on the Nile's east bank in Upper Egypt. His reign marks the beginning of the Middle Kingdom period. During this time, construction began on the Temple of Amun at Karnak.

An Asian people called the Hyksos came to power in the 1600s B.C. Egyptians learned much about the art of war from these foreign rulers. The Hyksos introduced horse-drawn chariots, bronze and iron swords, and other military gear.

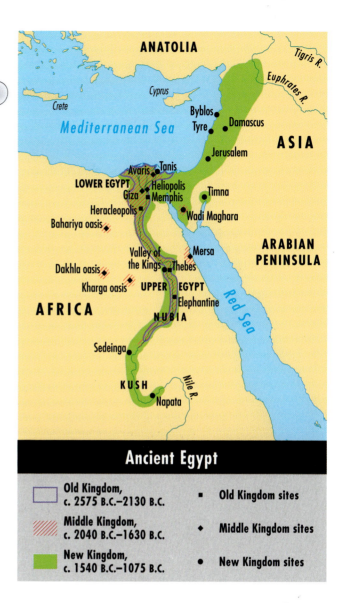

Ancient Egypt

- Old Kingdom, c. 2575 B.C.–2130 B.C.
- Middle Kingdom, c. 2040 B.C.–1630 B.C.
- New Kingdom, c. 1540 B.C.–1075 B.C.

- ▪ Old Kingdom sites
- ◆ Middle Kingdom sites
- ● New Kingdom sites

Major Periods in Ancient Egyptian History

c. 3100 B.C.	Egypt united by King Menes
c. 2575 B.C.–2130 B.C.	Old Kingdom
c. 2040 B.C.–1630 B.C.	Middle Kingdom
c. 1540 B.C.–1075 B.C.	New Kingdom
323 B.C.–30 A.D.	Ptolemaic period

The New Kingdom: Conquests and Construction

Ahmose, a Theban prince, drove the Hyksos out in the 1500s B.C. This began the New Kingdom period, with Thebes as the capital. With its new military skills, Egypt became a major power. Under Thutmose III, Egypt took over Nubia, Palestine, Syria, and northern Iraq. New lands meant new sources of wealth. Exotic woods, ivory, and precious metals and stones poured into the pharaohs' warehouses.

The tomb of Tutankhamun in the Valley of the Kings was discovered in 1922.

Hatshepsut, the Female Pharaoh

Hatshepsut was the daughter of Thutmose I and the wife of Thutmose II. When her husband died, his son and successor, Thutmose III, was still a child. Hatshepsut was expected to rule in the boy's place until he grew up, but she wanted more. She had herself crowned as the pharaoh and ruled for twenty-two years. In art, Hatshepsut is sometimes shown dressed as a male pharaoh. For her tomb, she built a magnificent temple at Deir el-Bahri near the Valley of the Kings. It was built into a solid stone mountainside.

To show off their power, New Kingdom pharaohs built huge temples, monuments, and statues of themselves. Ramses II was the greatest builder of all. He built the temples at Abu Simbel and enlarged the temple at Karnak. For their tombs, New Kingdom rulers built huge cities of the dead. These tomb sites were on the west bank of the Nile, across from Thebes. Today, they are named the Valley of the Kings, the Valley of the Queens, and the Tombs of the Nobles.

Ramses III of the Twentieth Dynasty was the last great New Kingdom pharaoh. In later dynasties, foreigners from Nubia, Libya, Ethiopia, and Assyria held the throne. Cambyses, the son of Persia's Cyrus the Great, invaded Egypt in 525 B.C., and Persian pharaohs ruled for the next two hundred years.

The Boy King

We know about Tutankhamun, or "King Tut," from his lavish tomb in the Valley of the Kings. Tutankhamun, the "boy king," reigned in the 1300s B.C. He died when he was about eighteen years old. More than five thousand objects were found in his tomb, including furniture, games, weapons, and a golden chariot. Among the clothes in his tomb were twenty-eight pairs of gloves and twenty-five head coverings.

Alexander and the Ptolemies

In 332 B.C., Alexander the Great marched into Egypt. Just twenty-four years old, Alexander already ruled the Greek Empire, and he would soon gain control of the Persian Empire. In Memphis, he was enthroned as pharaoh. He built his capital city on the Mediterranean coast and named it Alexandria. Alexander also paid a visit to the famous oracle, or fortune-teller, at Siwa. It was rumored the oracle declared Alexander a god.

Alexander died in 323 B.C. Before he died, Alexander divided his empire among his finest generals. Egypt went to Ptolemy, who installed himself as pharaoh. The Ptolemies reigned for the next three hundred years. During the Ptolemaic period, Greek culture dominated Egypt. Greek scholars and scientists made Alexandria the cultural capital of the Mediterranean. Astronomers, mathematicians, doctors, and engineers worked and studied there. Alexandria's library and museum had the most magnificent collection of manuscripts and documents in the world.

Across the Mediterranean from Egypt, another great empire was rising. The Roman Empire was spreading across southern Europe and into Asia. Naturally, the Romans turned their eyes to Egypt. For years, the Ptolemies paid exorbitant taxes to Rome. Cleopatra, the last Ptolemy ruler, paid, too. But she had a plan.

Cleopatra knew that Egypt was in grave danger. She also knew that Rome had become the greatest military power in the world. She believed her best chance to save her kingdom was to join forces with Rome. She befriended Julius Caesar, the Roman emperor, and they had a son. After Caesar was assassinated, she married one of his generals, Mark Antony. The marriage suited Mark Antony's ambitions, too. By combining his own forces with Egypt's, he could defeat his rival, Octavian, and then rule the whole Roman Empire.

A sculpture of Cleopatra, who reigned from 51 to 30 B.C.

Lighthouse to Ancient Mariners

In 1995, archaeologist Jean-Yves Empereur dredged up massive chunks of granite from the murky waters of Alexandria Bay. They turned out to be pieces of the world's first lighthouse, the legendary Pharos of Alexandria.

Built in the third century B.C., the Pharos was called one of the Seven Wonders of the Ancient World. It stood over 400 feet (120 m) high. A fire burned continuously from its peak, while a mirror reflected the light to ships as far as 70 miles (110 km) away.

An earthquake reduced the lighthouse to rubble in 1375. For more than six hundred years, the Pharos remained only a mysterious legend. "At last, we can put our finger on the myth," said Empereur.

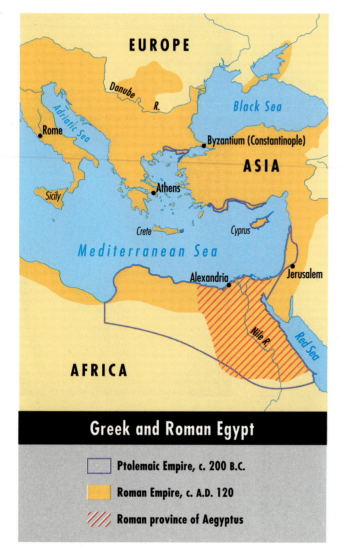

Greek and Roman Egypt

☐ Ptolemaic Empire, c. 200 B.C.

🟧 Roman Empire, c. A.D. 120

🟥 Roman province of Aegyptus

Things did not work out as they had planned. Octavian, who was later known as the emperor Augustus, conquered Egypt's forces at the sea battle of Actium in 31 B.C. He captured Alexandria the following year. Seeing that they had lost everything, Mark Antony and Cleopatra committed suicide, and Egypt became a Roman province. The days of the pharaohs were over.

Roman Rule

Life was rough for Egyptians under Roman rule. The Roman governors demanded huge taxes and forced Egyptian peasants to serve in the Roman army. Loads of grain from Egypt's farms were shipped to Rome.

In the first century A.D., Christianity sprang up in the Roman Empire. In Egypt, the Christian sect that developed was known as the Coptic Church. Roman emperors saw the new religion as a threat. They outlawed it and began executing Christians. In the third century, Emperor Diocletian had thousands of Egypt's Christians put to death. Later emperors reversed the rule. In A.D. 313, Emperor Constantine converted to Christianity, and it eventually became the Roman Empire's official religion.

In A.D. 395, the Roman Empire split in two. Rome was the capital of the Western Empire, and the Eastern, or Byzantine, Empire was ruled from Constantinople (now Istanbul, Turkey). Egypt became part of the Byzantine Empire. As the Byzantines weakened, Egypt became ripe for another takeover.

The Arab Invasion

Across the Red Sea in Arabia, Muhammad (570–632) was preaching the new religion of Islam. Muhammad's teachings spread like wildfire. His followers, called Muslims, conquered the whole of Arabia and moved north into Syria and Persia. In 639, the Arab army under Amr ibn al-As invaded Egypt, taking Cairo in 641 and Alexandria in 642. Ibn al-As built the walled military city of al-Fustat (Old Cairo) in 641.

Gradually, Arab ways mixed with local customs or replaced them altogether. The native Coptic language gave way to Arabic as Egypt's official tongue, and Islam became the official religion. The ancient cultures of the pharaohs, Persians, Greeks, and Romans all but disappeared.

The First Caliphs

After Muhammad's death, military and religious leaders called caliphs ruled Islamic lands. Armed with their beliefs, they fought each other for control of Muslim territory. At first, Egypt became a province under the Umayyad caliphs (661–750). Their capital was Damascus, in Syria. Abbasid caliphs took over Egypt in 750. They ruled their empire from Baghdad, in present-day Iraq.

The Fatimid dynasty established itself in Tunisia, a North African land west of Egypt, in 909. Jawhar, a great Fatimid general, occupied Egypt in 969. Caliph al-Muizz built al-Qahirah (Cairo) in 973 and made it his capital. From there, he conquered much of Arabia, Palestine, and Syria.

Egypt prospered under the Fatimids. Merchant ships from India and China brought goods to Alexandria and the Red Sea ports. Egypt then traded those goods with cities in Italy. Al-Azhar University was founded. Arts and literature flourished, and Cairo became a center of learning.

As Islam spread, the Christian Church watched its holy lands being taken over. Pope Urban II, the head of the Catholic Church, called upon Christians everywhere to fight Crusades, or holy wars, and regain what the Church thought of as Christian lands. In 1099, the Christians took control of the holy city of Jerusalem, in Palestine. In the 1100s, Crusaders marched against the Fatimids in Egypt. That paved the way for the Fatimids to fall to Saladin.

Saladin and the Ayyubids

Saladin is one of the most famous warriors in history. His Arabic name, Salah ad-Din, means "the bounty of religion." As a young man, Saladin studied religion in Damascus. When the Fatimids asked Syria for help against the Crusaders, he joined his uncle's army in Egypt. To Saladin and most Egyptians, the Abbasids were Egypt's rightful rulers. When the Fatimid caliph died in 1171, Saladin took over, and when the ruler of Syria died in 1174, Saladin annexed Syria, too.

As leader, or sultan, of Egypt and Syria, Saladin established the Ayyubid dynasty. Saladin's greatest goal still lay ahead—to drive the Crusaders out of Palestine and reunite Muslim lands. He went on to capture Jerusalem in 1187 and confined the Crusaders to a few coastal towns.

The Mamelukes

Ayyubid rulers surrounded themselves with a bevy of soldier-bodyguards called Mamelukes. The Mamelukes at first were slaves from Turkey, Greece, and central Asia. Mamelukes were taken as boys and trained to be soldiers and government officials. Once their training was over, they were free. Some held high positions and became very powerful.

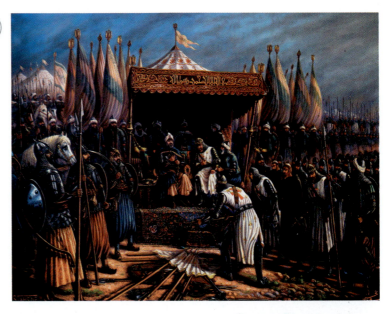

The Crusader Richard the Lionheart, king of England, surrendered to Saladin in 1187.

In 1250, the Mamelukes took control of Egypt. Mameluke merchants carried on trade with Europe and Asia. With their vast wealth, they supported beautiful architecture and fine pottery and metalwork. The Mamelukes' greatest leader was a general named Baybars. He drove invaders out of Palestine, took over Syria, and won many towns away from the Crusaders. In time, however, the Mameluke army split into rival groups and lost its fighting edge.

The Ottomans

Selim, a sultan of the Turkish Ottoman Empire, knew his well-equipped army had an unbeatable weapon—newly invented cannons. In 1517, Selim invaded Egypt, capturing Cairo and installing himself as caliph. Egypt remained a province of the Ottoman Empire for almost three hundred years. But while the Ottomans were officially in charge, the Mamelukes continued to serve as powerful local administrators. The Ottomans and the Mamelukes were in a constant struggle for power in Egypt. For more than two hundred years, this struggle played out in fighting, intrigue, and assassinations.

Napoleon and the French

Napoleon Bonaparte of France sailed a fleet of ships to Egypt's coast on July 1, 1798. France was about to take over much of western Europe, and Great Britain was one of France's greatest enemies. Napoleon wanted to seize Egypt in order to disrupt British trade with India. In the Battle of the Pyramids near Cairo, Napoleon conquered the Mameluke army and took control of Egypt. He organized a modern government, started irrigation projects, and planned a Suez canal route. French scholars and scientists studied Egypt's culture and farming practices. They also began to uncover the buried treasures of ancient Egypt.

Napoleon's Invasion of Egypt

→ British route   → French route
✸ British victory   ✸ French victory

Mediterranean Sea

Battle of the Nile
Rosetta
Aboukir Bay
Alexandria
El Rahmaniya
EGYPT
Cairo
Battle of the Pyramids
Nile R.

THE ROSETTA STONE

Champollion and the Rosetta Stone

In 1799, near the Egyptian town of Rosetta, a French officer discovered a slab of stone inscribed with three sets of writing. One set was hieroglyphic symbols, but no one knew how to read them. Their meaning was a mystery. The slab, named the Rosetta Stone, went to a museum. Finally in 1822, a French scholar named Jean-François Champollion cracked the mystery. Two of the inscriptions were in languages that he knew—Greek and demotic, a later form of Egyptian writing. To his surprise, the inscriptions said the same thing. By comparing the hieroglyphs to the other two writings, he developed a hieroglyphic "dictionary."

In 1799, Napoleon returned to France, leaving his generals to keep order. Now Great Britain saw its chance to get a foothold in Egypt. British troops joined forces with the Ottomans and Mamelukes. Together, they hammered away at the French until the French troops pulled out in 1801.

Muhammad Ali and His Successors

In the aftermath of the European war, Muhammad Ali, an Ottoman commander, gained control of Egypt. Muhammad Ali had learned a lot from watching the British and French. He realized that Europe was far ahead of Egypt in many ways. He immediately set to work modernizing the country. He brought in French military advisers to train his army. Factories were built to make textiles and process iron. Schools of medi-

The Curse of King Tut

Legend has it that an ancient curse guarded King Tut's tomb. After November 4, 1922, when British archaeologist Howard Carter discovered the tomb of King Tutankhamun, a deadly cholera epidemic broke out in Luxor. Then more than a dozen of Carter's friends died mysteriously after visiting the tomb. Carter's partner, Lord Carnarvon, was bitten by a mosquito as he left the site. The bite led to blood poisoning, and he too died.

Some say that the "curse" rumor was started by a newspaperman who was jealous that Carter had sold his story to a rival newspaper. Many scientists now believe the deaths were caused by bacteria or fungi from the tomb.

cine and engineering were opened, and European scholars came to lecture. Bright young Egyptians studied in Europe and then came back and translated their textbooks into Arabic. Gradually, Muhammad Ali and his successors made Egypt independent of the Ottoman Empire.

Muhammad Ali's son, Said Pasha, ruled Egypt from 1854 to 1863. He granted a French company the right to build a canal from the Mediterranean to the Gulf of Suez. The Suez Canal opened in 1869. Said's nephew Ismail improved Egypt's schools, roads, railroads, and factories. But his lavish spending on these projects, as well as on palaces and other luxuries, cast Egypt deep into debt. In 1875, to raise money, Ismail sold Egypt's shares in the Suez Canal to Great Britain, making France and Britain the canal's primary owners.

British Rule

Fed up with foreign interference, Egyptians rebelled in 1882. But British forces subdued the rebels and occupied the country. When World War I (1914–1918) broke out, the British declared Egypt a protectorate of the British Empire. This implied that the British were protecting Egypt. In reality, they were protecting the Suez Canal.

In 1922, the British granted limited independence to Egypt. The British installed a king, Fu'ad I, but in fact they continued to run much of the country's affairs. The British army stayed for World War II (1939–1945), again to protect the canal. In 1942, German and Italian forces landed on Egypt's Mediterranean coast. At the two-week-long Battle of el-Alamein, the British forced the invaders to retreat.

After the war, the United Nations divided Palestine to make a homeland for Jewish people. Egypt and other Arab countries protested, but the Jewish state of Israel became a reality in 1948. Conflict between Israel and the Arab states continues to this day.

British troops fight in the Battle of el-Alamein to protect the Suez Canal in 1942.

President Gamal Abdel Nasser was a strong believer in Pan-Arabism. He thought Arab countries should work together in ways that would benefit them all.

After centuries of outside rule, Egyptians were ready to take control of their own country. On July 23, 1952, army officers led by Gamal Abdel Nasser overthrew King Farouk. Egypt was declared a republic in 1953, and Nasser became prime minister the next year. That same year, the British agreed to remove all their forces from Egypt. In 1956, Nasser took over the presidency.

Nasser tried to solve many of the problems that troubled his country. He urged rural people to stay in their villages and affirm their Egyptian identity. New laws gave more agricultural laborers a chance to own land. Public schools were improved, and graduates were given government jobs.

Nasser also wanted to build the Aswan High Dam, but he needed money to do it. The United States and Britain at first agreed to lend the money, but later withdrew the offer. Nasser responded in 1956 by taking control of the Suez Canal, which was then under British and French control. Tolls from the canal would pay for the dam. This move made him a hero in the Arab world. Nasser then took over Egypt's banks and private industries. Nearly 250,000 foreigners were required to leave the country.

Meanwhile, Israelis and Palestinian Arabs were in constant conflict. In June 1967, Egypt closed the Gulf of Aqaba to

Israeli ships. Israel then stormed into several Arab countries, including Egypt, Syria, and Jordan, and occupied the Sinai in the Six-Day War. Israel's victory humiliated Egypt and other Arab states.

Sadat and Middle East Peace

After President Nasser's death in 1970, Anwar Sadat became president. He reopened Egypt's doors to foreign businesses to help the economy. His main concern, however, was Israel.

In October 1973, Sadat sent troops across the Suez Canal in an effort to win back the Sinai, which was occupied by Israel. In the eighteen days of fighting, called the October War, not much was accomplished. Hoping to make peace, Sadat visited Israeli prime minister Menachem Begin in 1977. The following year, Sadat and Begin met in the United States and signed the Camp David Accords. The two shared the 1978 Nobel Peace Prize for their efforts. The following year, the longtime enemies signed a peace treaty, and the Sinai was restored to Egypt.

Anwar Sadat (left) shakes hands with Israeli prime minister Menachem Begin and U.S. president Jimmy Carter after signing a peace treaty.

Land of the Pharaohs **61**

In October 1981, Sadat was shot dead. The assassins were members of al-Jihad, a Muslim fundamentalist group. Vice President Hosni Mubarak then became president.

Like Sadat, President Mubarak chose a path of tolerance and moderation, although he did not feel he could allow full democracy in Egypt. He took an active role in the Middle East peace process, calling together many peace conferences of Middle Eastern leaders. At home, Mubarak's economic reforms made Egypt stronger and wealthier. He began turning government-run businesses over to private ownership.

Mubarak's most difficult task has been combating terrorism. He firmly believes that Egypt should have a secular, open society. This is directly opposed to the strict views of Islamic fundamentalist groups. In response to Murbarak's differing views, terrorists carried out bomb attacks in Cairo and Luxor in 1997, killing dozens of people. Mubarak responded with crackdowns on terrorist leaders and organizations.

Mubarak's friendship with the United States has angered fundamentalist groups even more. Along with most other Arabs, these groups oppose both the U.S. alliance with Israel and U.S. actions in the Arab world. The United States invaded Iraq in 2003 and overthrew dictator Saddam Hussein. The invasion brought on a wave of demonstrations in Egypt. It brought more violence, too. In 2004, 2005, and 2006, terrorists bombed several resort towns on the Sinai Peninsula.

Mubarak walks a fine line between his position as an Arab leader and his vision of tolerance. Should Egypt hold more

firmly to its Islamic roots? Or should it take a stand for openness and compromise? This will be Egypt's greatest challenge in the years ahead.

Thousand of Egyptians protest the approaching U.S. invasion of Iraq in March 2003.

Governing Egypt

THE ARAB REPUBLIC OF EGYPT ADOPTED ITS PRESENT constitution in 1971. Like the United States and Canada, Egypt has three branches of government. The president heads the executive branch. The People's Assembly is the legislative, or lawmaking, branch. Egypt's court system makes up the judicial branch.

In Egypt, the president plays a strong role in the national government. He sets government policies and commands the armed forces. The president may appoint one or more vice presidents, although Hosni Mubarak has never appointed one. The president also appoints a prime minister and a council of ministers. Ministers must be at least thirty-five years old. The president chooses many local officials, too.

The Egyptian president must be a man at least forty years old and born of Egyptian parents. The president is elected to a six-year term, and there is no limit on the number of terms he can serve. Officially, the People's Assembly is supposed to nominate a candidate for president who is then approved by the people. In fact, however, Gamal Abdel Nasser, Anwar Sadat, and Hosni Mubarak all came to the presidency without going through

Opposite: **The central government office building, El-Mugamma, in Cairo**

Women in Egypt gained the right to vote in 1956.

this complete process. Mubarak, who has been president since 1981, has not allowed any real challenge to his rule.

In 2005, the constitution was amended to change the electoral process. The amendment paved the way for candidates of many parties to run for president and for voters to elect the president directly. Egyptians welcomed the change as a step toward democracy, but most doubted that these reforms would make a significant difference in the outcome of future elections.

The People's Assembly and the Shura Council

The People's Assembly is Egypt's lawmaking body. It has a total of 454 members. At least half the assembly members must come from the laborer and farmer classes, and some members must be women. The president appoints ten of the members. The other 444 members are elected by popular vote.

The People's Assembly in session

Voters in each of 222 districts elect two members per district. The entire People's Assembly is elected at one time, and its members serve a five-year term.

The 264-member Shura Council studies national issues and drafts proposals and laws. It advises the president and the People's Assembly, although it has no lawmaking power. The president appoints one-third

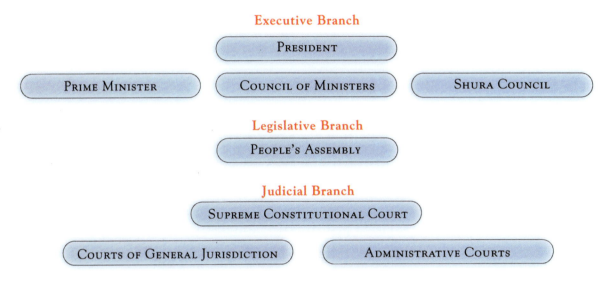

NATIONAL GOVERNMENT OF EGYPT

Executive Branch

PRESIDENT

PRIME MINISTER   COUNCIL OF MINISTERS   SHURA COUNCIL

Legislative Branch

PEOPLE'S ASSEMBLY

Judicial Branch

SUPREME CONSTITUTIONAL COURT

COURTS OF GENERAL JURISDICTION   ADMINISTRATIVE COURTS

of its members, and voters elect the others. Shura Council members serve six-year terms.

The Courts

Egypt's judicial branch is in theory independent of the other branches. The Supreme Constitutional Court is Egypt's highest court. Its judges review the laws to make sure they are in line with the constitution. They also resolve conflicts between lower courts. When two courts make opposite decisions, the Supreme Court makes a ruling.

There are two types of lower courts: courts of general jurisdiction and administrative courts. The highest court of general jurisdiction is the court of cassation. It hears disputed cases from courts of appeal. Below the courts of appeal are

The National Flag

Egypt's flag features three horizontal bands—red, white, and black. These are traditional Arab colors. The red band represents Egypt's history before it became a republic; white stands for Egypt's peaceful revolution in 1952; and black stands for the end of the Egyptian people's oppression. In the center of the white band is the crest of Saladin, Egypt's national emblem. It is a golden hawk and shield with a scroll underneath.

tribunals of first instance and district courts. Judges decide all court cases in Egypt. There are no trials by jury.

Local Government

Egypt is divided into twenty-six *muhafazat,* or governorates. The national government appoints a governor to each one. Five of the governorates are actually large cities: Cairo, Alexandria, Suez, Ismailia, and Port Said. Each governorate is divided into districts. Within the districts are towns and villages, each with a mayor and local councils. The local councils oversee such areas as education, health care, housing, and farming.

Religion and the Government

According to Egypt's constitution, Islam is the national religion. The Islamic code of law (*Shari'a*) is a guiding principle for Egyptian law. At the same time, freedom of worship is guaranteed for people of other faiths.

The National Anthem

Egypt's national anthem, "Biladi" ("My Homeland"), was adopted in 1979. Sayed Darwish, a pioneer of Arab music, wrote the words and music in the early 1900s.

Arabic version

Biladi biladi biladi

Laki hubbi wa fuadi.

Biladi biladi biladi

Laki hubbi wa fuadi.

Misr ya umm al bilad

Inti ghayati wal murad

Wa 'ala kull il 'ibad

Kam lineelik min ayadi.

Misr inti aghla durra

Fawq gabeen ad-dahr ghurra

Ya biladi 'aishi hurra

Wa as 'adi ragh-al-adi.

Misr awladik kiram

Aufiya yar'u-ziman

Saufa takhti bil-maram

Bittihadhim wa-ittihadi.

English translation

My homeland, my homeland, my homeland,

My love and heart are for thee.

My homeland, my homeland, my homeland,

My love and heart are for thee.

Egypt! O mother of all lands,

My hope and my ambition,

How can one count

The blessings of the Nile for mankind?

Egypt! Most precious jewel,

Shining on the brow of eternity!

O my homeland, be forever free,

Safe from every foe!

Egypt! Noble are thy children,

Loyal, and guardians of thy soil.

In war and peace

We give our lives for thy sake.

Legal questions concerning marriage and family are decided by the religious law of the people involved. For most Egyptians, this is Islamic law. Christians and Jews resolve these issues within their own religious communities.

One of the most explosive issues in Egypt today is the "political Islam" movement. This is a campaign to make Egypt an Islamic state governed by Islamic law. The government favors a more moderate path. This creates conflict in many areas of

Days before the September 2005 presidential elections, supporters of President Hosni Murabak cheer as he arrives at a rally in Cairo.

Egyptian life. Fundamentalists want Islamic law to dominate Egypt's arts, culture, education, and lifestyles. Women's clothing is one example. Fundamentalists insist that women in Egypt should wear a veil that covers most of the body. But the government continues to allow more liberal dress.

Political Parties

Political parties were outlawed in 1953. The ban was lifted in 1977. Since then, strict laws have controlled the formation of political parties. In 2005, there were fourteen official parties.

The National Democratic Party (NDP) is Egypt's major political party. It was founded by Anwar Sadat in 1978, and it has dominated the government ever since. Typically, NDP members hold more than three-quarters of the seats in the People's Assembly. Since 1981, Hosni Mubarak, as party leader, has won the presidency in one election after another. Most Egyptians believe the votes are not counted fairly.

The NDP's main official rivals are the New Wafd Party and the National Progressive Unionist Party. Unofficial rivals pose a greater threat to the NDP, however. By law, no party can be based solely on religious issues. That eliminates Egypt's Islamic fundamentalist groups, who want to reshape Egypt as an Islamic society ruled by Islamic law. But one of these groups, the Muslim Brotherhood, has made headway in the political system.

Formed in 1928, the Muslim Brotherhood was banned in 1954. But it has found ways to gain power over the years. In some elections, the Brotherhood has won seats in the People's Assembly by forming alliances with approved parties. Individual members have also won seats by running as independents. Members of the Muslim Brotherhood won seventeen seats in the 2000 elections. They formed the largest block among independents, as well as the largest group opposing the NDP. More victories are expected in the future.

Political Terrorism

Some Islamic fundamentalists in Egypt have formed violent terrorist groups such as Islamic Jihad, or al-Jihad (Holy Struggle). Some terrorists aim to overthrow President Mubarak's government. Others cannot tolerate Israel's policies toward the Palestinians. Members of various groups have killed tourists and Egyptian officials, hijacked airplanes, bombed buildings, and tried to assassinate Mubarak. Even the Muslim Brotherhood condemns these terrorist attacks.

The Egyptian government has cracked down hard on terrorism. Police actively seek out terrorists, and many have been jailed or executed.

Cairo: Did You Know This?

Cairo, Egypt's capital, is the largest city in Africa, with an estimated population of 7,438,376 in 2005. That makes it one of the fifteen largest cities in the world. More than fifteen million people are packed into the metropolitan area, which is one of the world's most densely populated areas.

Cairo straddles the Nile River and includes two islands—Gezira and Roda. Bridges connect the riverbanks and the islands. Even on a quick tour through the Cairo area, a visitor sees monuments from five thousand years of Egypt's history. The most modern sections of Cairo lie close to the Nile. Near the east bank is the main business section, the Egyptian Museum, and the government building. The Opera House/Cultural Center and the 614-foot (187 m) Cairo Tower stand on Gezira Island. To the northeast, a huge statue of Ramses II towers over the main railway station.

East of the city center is Khan al-Khalili souq,

or market. Merchants have sold their wares there since the Fatimid dynasty in the 900s. South of the market are some of Egypt's grandest Muslim sites, including the Mosque of Ibn Tulun, the Ottoman mosque of Muhammad Ali, the Citadel of Saladin, and the *madrasa* (religious school) of Mameluke Sultan Hassan.

Old Cairo, to the south, is the oldest section of town. It contains the Roman Fortress of Babylon, the Coptic Museum, and many Coptic Christian churches. Looming west of Cairo are the pyramids of Giza. They are close enough to be seen clearly from the windows of many Cairo office buildings.

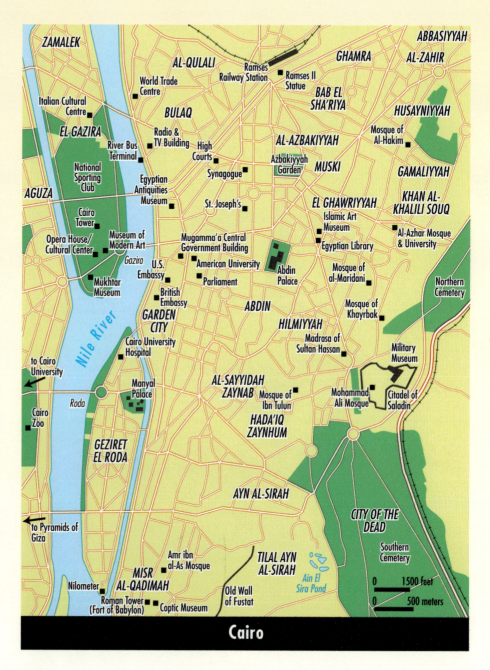

Cairo

Fruits of
Their Labor

Oil refineries dot the Red Sea coast.

Economically, Egypt faces a number of problems. It has to import food to feed its large population. It is not exporting as much oil as it once did. It has high inflation and unemployment. Economic reforms begun in the 1990s are intended to address some of these problems.

The major reform program has been privatization—selling government-owned industries to private companies. The government has sold power plants, roads, airports, banks, hotels, and many other businesses. Private industries tend to be more flexible. They produce more and make more money. Other reforms have included irrigating the Western Desert, building new cities, developing the Mediterranean coastal strip, and building an underground transit system.

Opposite: **A father and son work the fields near the Giza pyramids.**

More than one-third of Egyptian workers make their living by farming. Many work the land by hand because their farms are too small for large machines. Crops can grow on only about 4 percent of Egypt's land. But water, plus year-round warm weather, makes the farms highly productive. Almost all the farmland is in the Nile Delta and the Nile River valley. Some desert regions are being developed for farming. Other farmland is disappearing as urban areas grow.

Egypt leads the world in producing long-fibered cotton, its principal crop. The most important food crops are grains such as rice, barley, wheat, and corn. Other important crops are onions, beans, tomatoes, and oranges. Sugarcane and dates grow all year. Egypt is the world's top producer of dates. In some fields, date palms are used as shade for other crops, such as cabbage. After the dates are harvested, they are spread out on the ground to dry.

Farmers harvest sugarcane in Luxor.

The construction of the Aswan High Dam enabled Egyptian farmers to increase the number of crops they could grow in a year.

Growing Seasons and Irrigation Methods

In ancient times, Egypt had two growing seasons. Now, thanks to the Aswan High Dam, farmers are able to plant three seasons of crops. The summer season—from March to November—is the time for cotton, tomatoes, corn, rice, and

Moving the Water

The *shadoof*, or watersweep, is a four-thousand-year-old method of drawing water from a river. A long pole with a weight on one end is mounted on the bank. At the other end is a goatskin bag or bucket, which is lowered into the water. The weighted pole then moves like a seesaw, slinging the water container onto the shore.

potatoes. October through April is the main season, the time for growing wheat, barley, beans, onions, and bersim—a clover for animal feed. The Nile used to flood from July through October, but the Aswan High Dam controls the floodwaters, so that time is used as an extra growing season.

Pumping stations pump Nile water into wide irrigation canals along the bank. Smaller canals branch off from the main channel. Every three weeks, the canal gates are opened to flood the fields.

A gigantic irrigation project is under way in the Western Desert. It involves building a canal from the Nile to the New Valley oases. Irrigating the New Valley has been a dream since ancient times when a branch of the Nile once flowed through the area.

What Egypt Grows, Makes, and Mines

Agriculture (2003 est.)

Sugarcane	16,334,800 metric tons
Wheat	6,844,700 metric tons
Cotton	200,000 metric tons

Manufacturing (1999–2000 est.)

Petroleum fuels	19,705,000 metric tons
Cement	18,932,000 metric tons
Cottonseed oil	260,000 metric tons

Mining (2002 est.)

Petroleum	274,000,000 metric tons
Natural gas	31,000,000 metric tons
Iron ore	2,300,000 metric tons

Money Facts

The Egyptian pound (£E) is Egypt's standard of currency. One pound is divided into 100 piasters. Banknotes come in values of £E 1, 5, 10, 20, 50, 100, 500, and 1,000. The larger the banknote, the larger its value. Egypt also issues 25- and 50-piaster bills. There are 25- and 50-piaster coins, too, but they are rarely used. In April 2006, US$1 was equal to £E 5.75, and £E 1 was equal to US$0.17.

Egyptian banknotes are printed in Arabic on one side and English on the other. The Arabic side features famous mosques. The English side shows pictures of antiquities such as the Sphinx, the temple at Abu Simbel, and the mask of Tutankhamun.

Manufacturing

Egypt's most important industries are processed foods and cotton textiles. Textile plants spin cotton fibers into thread and yarn, weave cotton into cloth, and make finished clothing. Cotton yarn and fabric are Egypt's major exports after petroleum products. Other manufactured goods include cements, chemicals, fertilizers, drugs, and steel.

In the past, the government built and owned most factories. This system is gradually changing. More and more factories are jointly owned by the government and private companies.

Factory workers process tea in Alexandria.

Nile Fishing

Fishing on the Nile is a culture of its own. Fishing families live and work on their boats. To catch fish from the boat, a child casts a net into the water as a grown-up rows. Then, as they drift around in a circular pattern, the net fills with fish. Nile perch, tilapia, and catfish are some of the fish commonly caught in the Nile.

Mining

Thousands of years ago, Egypt's pharaohs used mining to increase their wealth. Gold, turquoise, and granite are among the treasures in Egypt's quarries and mines.

Today, petroleum and natural gas are Egypt's richest mineral resources. In 2003, Egypt was producing about 750,000 barrels of oil a day. Petroleum products make up about one-third of Egypt's exports. The natural gas industry is booming.

About 50 percent of oil produced in Egypt comes from the Gulf of Suez.

The Arab Gas Pipeline opened in 2003. It carries natural gas from Egypt to Jordan.

Huge offshore oil rigs operate in the Gulf of Suez, Egypt's major oil-producing region. The Western Desert also has large natural gas and oil deposits. More oil and gas have been found near Giza and Port Said. Other important minerals in Egypt include iron ore, phosphates, manganese, uranium, and coal.

Tourism

Tourism is one of Egypt's major sources of income. Tourists pour into Egypt to see the Great Pyramid and the Sphinx. Around Luxor, they marvel at the Valley of the Kings and the temples at Karnak and Thebes. Near Aswan, they visit the Temples of Philae and Ramses II.

Cruises in "floating hotels" are popular, too. These luxurious boats take visitors up the Nile, stopping at ancient sites along the way. Tourist villages operate along the Red Sea coasts at Hurghada and in the Sinai.

In the 1990s, terrorist groups began attacking tourists. This was a blow for Egypt's tourism industry. Thanks to the government's stern measures, tourism has been recovering.

Resources

Legend		
Cash crops and mixed cereals	Al Aluminum	K Potassium
Cotton and cereals	Au Gold	Mn Manganese
Nomadic livestock herding	C Coal	NG Natural gas
Nonagricultural land	Cem Cement	P Phosphates
Oases	Fe Iron	S Sulfur
	Gyp Gypsum	
Hydroelectric power	Oil	

Commuters in Cairo travel
by foot, train, bus, and car.

Traveling by Land

Only about 3 percent of Egyptians own cars, although this may be hard to believe when you are driving in Cairo. The streets are thick with traffic. People also travel on buses, taxis, motorcycles, and bicycles. And even in Cairo, camels and donkey carts are part of the traffic flow.

With more than 31,000 miles (50,000 km) of paved roads, travel throughout Egypt is easy. Signposts are in Arabic and English, and distances are shown in kilometers. To cross the Suez Canal, motorists drive underneath it in the Ahmad Hamdi road tunnel. But travelers must plan ahead. Traffic to the tunnel can be heavy, stalls are common, and the tunnel closes at night.

Egypt's main railway line runs from Alexandria to Aswan—almost the entire length of the country. Cairo's subway, which opened in 1987, was Africa's first underground railway system. It has several stations in central Cairo and others in outlying areas.

Water and Air Travel

Egyptians travel and transport goods on the Nile, just as their ancestors have done for thousands of years. Besides the river system, Egypt has hundreds of miles of canals. Passenger ferries sail between Egyptian ports and Italy, Greece, Cyprus, and Aqaba, Jordan.

A ferry boat transports people across the Nile at Aswan.

For international trade, ships use the Mediterranean Sea, the Red Sea, and—connecting them—the Suez Canal. The canal is just over 100 miles (160 km) long. More than seventeen thousand ships pass through the Suez every year. Egypt gets a great deal of income from shipping through the Suez Canal, as ships pay a fee to pass through. Alexandria, on the Mediterranean, is the nation's major port. Others are Port Said and Damietta on the Mediterranean and Suez and Safraga on the Red Sea.

Most of the world's major airlines fly into Cairo's international airport at Heliopolis. Alexandria, Aswan, Hurghada, Luxor, and Sharm el-Sheikh have international airports, too. Small airlines fly to many popular locations within the country.

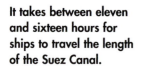

It takes between eleven and sixteen hours for ships to travel the length of the Suez Canal.

A man in Cairo reads one of Egypt's many newspapers.

Communications

Most of Egypt's publishing and broadcasting is centered in Cairo. The most important of the nation's seventeen daily newspapers are *al-Ahram* (the *Pyramids*), *al-Akhbar* (the *News*), and *al-Jumhuriyah* (the *Republic*). The *Egyptian Gazette* and *al-Ahram Weekly* are English-language papers.

The Egyptian Radio and Television Union (ERTU) controls Egypt's radio and television service. Satellites beam Egyptian programs to the rest of the Arab world, as well as to Great Britain and the United States. Egyptian television and films are popular wherever Arabic is spoken.

Except in the Western Desert oases, Egypt's telephone service is good. But many people who don't have home phones rely on cell phones. In 2005, about 9.6 million regular telephones were in use in Egypt. At the same time, there were 8.6 million cell phones. Internet use is widespread in Egypt, too. About 4.2 million Egyptians were Internet users in 2005.

Crowded Cities, Common Bonds

EGYPT HAS THE SECOND-HIGHEST POPULATION OF ALL African nations, after Nigeria. In 2005, Egypt's population was estimated at about 77.5 million. About 99 percent of Egypt's people live along the Nile or beside the Suez Canal, making these areas among the most densely populated in the world. Cairo and Alexandria are the largest cities.

Small communities are clustered around the desert oases. The government is trying to attract more settlers to desert areas, but people keep moving to the cities for jobs and a better standard of living. There is a saying that every minute

Opposite: **A bustling street in the oldest district of Cairo**

The al-Asafirah district is in Alexandria. The city's population of nearly 3.7 million is more than ten times what it was a hundred years ago.

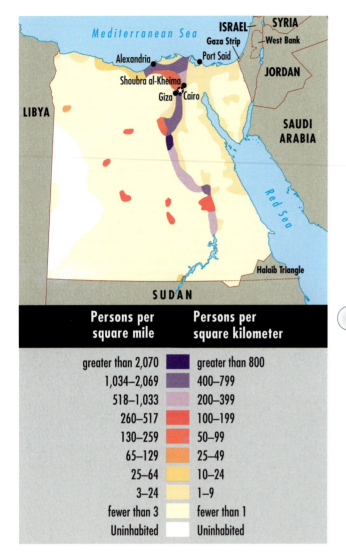

Persons per square mile	Persons per square kilometer
greater than 2,070	greater than 800
1,034–2,069	400–799
518–1,033	200–399
260–517	100–199
130–259	50–99
65–129	25–49
25–64	10–24
3–24	1–9
fewer than 3	fewer than 1
Uninhabited	Uninhabited

Population of Major Cities (2005 est.)

Cairo	7,438,376
Alexandria	3,693,412
Giza	2,541,837
Shoubra al-Kheima	1,021,862
Port Said	533,299
Suez	508,350

in Cairo, one person is born and two arrive by train.

The Sinai Peninsula is lightly populated. Many of its residents live along the Mediterranean and Red Sea coasts. Nomadic Bedouins live in the interior. They travel by camel and graze their goats and sheep on the scrubby vegetation.

Population Growth Problems

Egypt's population grows by more than one million people every year. This worsens problems of poverty, unemployment, housing shortages, and poor nutrition. Though conservative Islamic groups oppose family planning, the government has made efforts to educate people about birth control. As a result, between 1985 and 2005, Egypt's rate of growth slowed from 3 percent to 1.8 percent a year.

Feeding all the people is a major problem in overpopulated Egypt. Experts say that more farmland is now used to grow food for animals than food for people. This is because beef and chicken have become increasingly popular among middle- and upper-class Egyptians, so feed must be grown.

Who Are the Egyptians?

As a rule, Egyptians think of themselves as Arabs, but there is no single Egyptian "type." Over the centuries, native Egyptians mixed with a huge variety of people—Arabs, Berbers, Ethiopians, Persians, Turks, central Asians, Greeks, and Romans. In the south, some have blended with the Nubians of northern Sudan.

Farmers who live in rural villages along the Nile are called *fellahin*. Many raise crops using ancient methods and the tools of their ancestors. The standard of living among the fellahin is low. Their average monthly income is less than fifty U.S. dollars.

Minority groups in Egypt include Copts, Bedouins, and Nubians. Among the many foreign nationals living in Egypt are British, Greek, and Italian people.

Copts are not an ethnic minority, but a religious minority. They are the direct descendants

Who Lives in Egypt?

Arabs (including Bedouins)	99%
Nubians and foreign nationals (including Greek, Italian, French, and others)	1%

Children of the fellahin work the family land as soon as they are old enough.

A Nubian woman sells brightly colored scarves.

of Egyptians who lived in the days of the pharaohs. At the time of the Arab conquest, Copts formed the Christian majority. Over time, many converted from the Coptic Church to Islam. Today, some Copts are well-educated professionals, while others are terribly poor.

Bedouins form a small minority of Egypt's population. They are traditionally a nomadic people, although many have settled down to a farming lifestyle. Bedouins live throughout the Middle East—not only in Egypt, but also in Saudi Arabia, Jordan, and Israel. They think of themselves as Bedouins and Arabs, rather than as citizens of one particular country. Bedouins were the original people of the Sinai, and most Sinai residents today are Bedouins. Other Bedouins live in the Western and Eastern deserts.

Nubians are dark-skinned, non-Arab people. Pharaohs of the Twenty-fifth Dynasty were Nubian kings. Traditionally, Nubians lived along the Nile south of Aswan and in northern Sudan. Many lost their homes when the Aswan High Dam was built. Some moved north, while others stayed in the Lake Nasser area.

Arabic Language and Writing

While Arabic is Egypt's official language, many educated Egyptians also speak English or French. The Arabic language has several forms. Classical Arabic is a complex language used in fine literature such as the Qur'an, Islam's holy book. Modern standard Arabic, which includes many new words taken from other cultures, is used in business and for radio and television news. At home or on the streets, people use local dialects. These can be very different from one region to another. Cairo's dialect is the most widespread.

Common Arabic Words and Phrases

Yes	*Aywa* (EYE-wah)
No	*La*
Hello	*Assalaamu aleikum* (ah-sah-LA-moo ah-LAY-koom)
(*response to*) Hello	*Wa aleikum assalaam* (WAH ah-LAY-koom ah-sah-LAHM)
Good-bye	*Ma salaama* (MAH sah-LAH-mah)
Please (to a woman)	*Minfadlik* (min-FAHD-lik)
Please (to a man)	*Minfadlak* (min-FAHD-lahk)
Thank you	*Shukran* (shoo-KRAHN)
No, thank you	*La shukran* (LA shoo-KRAHN)
Where is . . . ?	*Feyn . . . ?* (FAYN)
How much?	*Bekaam?* (beh-KAHM)

The Arabic Alphabet

a	ا	d*	ض
b	ب	t*	ط
t	ت	z*	ظ
th	ث	a pause	ع
g	ج	gh	غ
h	ح	f	ف
kh	خ	q	ق
d	د	k	ك
dh	ذ	l	ل
r	ر	m	م
z	ز	n	ن
s	س	h	ه
sh	ش	w	و
s*	ص	y	ي

*Harder sounds

Many signs in Egypt include English or French for travelers who cannot read Arabic.

Arabic script is based on the alphabet of an ancient people called the Nabataeans. It is written from right to left. Arabic writings can be so decorative that they are considered art. The modern Arabic alphabet has twenty-eight characters—all consonants. Vowel sounds for *a*, *i*, and *u* are indicated by signs above or below a character. The numbers used in the Western world—called Arabic numerals—are derived from Arabic numbers.

Coptic Language and Writing

The Coptic language comes from ancient Egyptian. It grew out of the language spoken there between 2,000 and 2,500 years ago. At the time of the Arab invasion, Coptic was Egypt's everyday language. Then for many years, both Arabic and Coptic were commonly spoken. By the 1600s, spoken Coptic survived only in remote villages. The language is preserved today in Coptic Christian religious services.

Worshippers attend Mass in a Coptic church.

Coptic writing had a history of its own. Ancient hieroglyphic writing changed into a script called demotic. When the Ptolemies came to power, Egyptians began writing the Coptic language with the Greek alphabet, adding seven demotic letters. In the 300s, Copts translated the Bible from Greek into Coptic, and written Coptic took its final form. Coptic monks continue to preserve the script in prayer books.

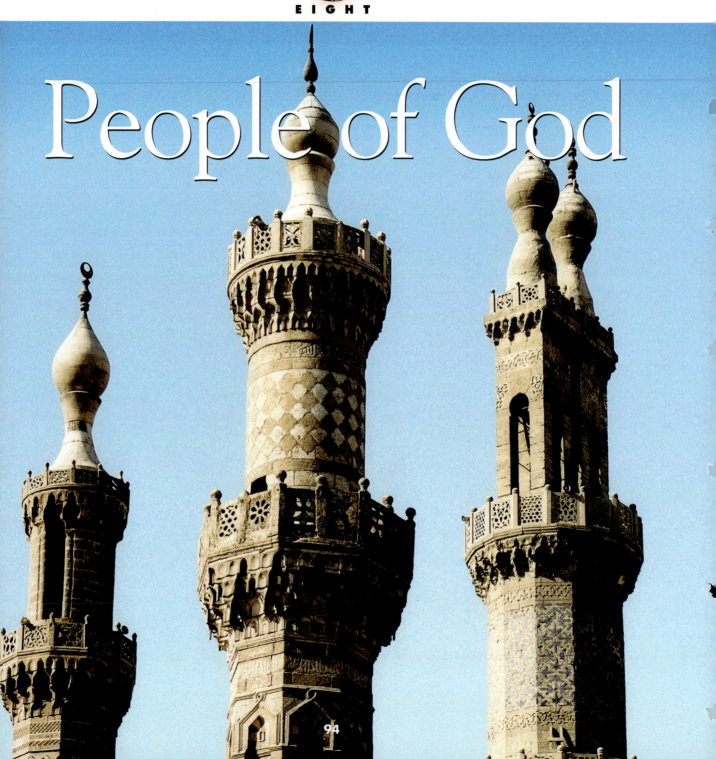

People of God

94

Islam is Egypt's official religion, though people of other religions are free to practice their faith. More than 90 percent of Egyptians follow Islam. Most Egyptian Muslims belong to the Sunni branch of Islam.

Islam, which means "submission," is the religion of the entire Arab world. A follower of Islam is called a Muslim, meaning "one who submits to the will of God." For Muslims, God's name is Allah. A common Muslim prayer goes, "There is no God but Allah, and Muhammad is the Prophet of Allah."

Opposite: **The minarets of the Al-Azhar Mosque in Cairo**

Young Egyptian Muslims visit the Muhammad Ali Mosque in Cairo.

Muhammad, who is called the Prophet, was the founder of Islam. His teachings were written down in the Qur'an, Islam's holy book. Islamic teachings cover every aspect of daily life—food, clothing, education, and manners.

When Muslims worship in mosques, they leave their shoes at the door. A muezzin calls the faithful to prayer from the minaret, the mosque's tower. Five times a day, wherever they are, devout Muslims kneel to pray, facing the holy city of Mecca in Saudi Arabia. In most Islamic cities today, loudspeakers broadcast the call to prayer.

Worshippers gather at the Al-Azhar Mosque in Cairo. The mosque dates back to 972.

All faithful Muslims practice the Five Pillars of Faith: (1) believing in Allah as the one God and in Muhammad as his prophet; (2) praying five times a day while facing the holy city of Mecca; (3) giving aid to the needy; (4) fasting during the month of Ramadan; and (5) making a pilgrimage to Mecca at least once in their lives.

The Islamic Calendar

Muslims divide the year into twelve months of twenty-nine or thirty days each, following cycles of the moon. Islamic astronomers determine the first day of each month. In different parts of the world, "first days" can be a day apart, because the moon is seen rising at different times.

The Islamic year is 354 days long (355 in leap years)—eleven days shorter than a year according to the Western calendar. So each year, feast days fall eleven days earlier than in the year before. "Year zero" in the Islamic calendar is A.D. 622. That was the year of the *hegira*, Muhammad's flight from Mecca to Medina to avoid persecution.

Inshallah

Has the fever passed? *Inshallah* (insh-AH-lah). Will you get to Cairo tomorrow? Inshallah. Will the beans be ready by dinnertime? Inshallah. In Egypt, as in much of the Islamic world, many questions are answered with *Inshallah*, meaning "God willing" or "If it pleases God." This expresses the belief that, regardless of the efforts of human beings, things happen only if God wills them.

Ramadan and Other Festivals

The month of Ramadan is Egypt's most festive season. During Ramadan, Muslims celebrate Muhammad's receiving the Qur'an from God. All monthlong, they fast from sunup to sundown, taking neither food nor water during the day. In Cairo, a cannon fires from the Citadel of Saladin at sunset, announcing that it is time for *iftar*, the feast that breaks the fast.

A traditional iftar begins with dates and apricots. Then comes lentil soup, meat pies, vegetables, and pastries. Feasting and parties go on through the night. Strings of lights and lanterns brighten the streets, and boys shoot off firecrackers. At sunrise, the fasting begins again. Ramadan is also a time for

Muhammad, the Prophet

Muhammad, who was born in 570, was a merchant in the Arabian city of Mecca. At the time, the scattered tribes of Arabia had a variety of local gods. Muslims believe that, one day, the angel Gabriel appeared to Muhammad in the desert. He told Muhammad to teach people to worship the one and only God, whose name is Allah. Muhammad is supposed to have received messages from God for the next twenty-two years. The Qur'an is the collection of these revelations.

Powerful people in Mecca were angered at Muhammad's teachings. In 622, they drove him out, and he fled to the city of Medina, in what is now Saudi Arabia. His flight, called the hegira, is marked as the beginning of Islam. In Medina, Muhammad gained many followers, and the new religion began to spread. Muhammad died in 632 in Medina.

exchanging good wishes and being especially generous to the poor. The feast of 'Id al-Fitr marks the end of Ramadan.

Other important festivals are Ras al-Sana al-Hegira (the Islamic new year) and 'Id al-Adha (Abraham's sacrifice). Some holidays are *moulids*, festivals honoring a holy person. Moulid an-Nabi, Muhammad's birthday, is celebrated across the Islamic world. In Cairo, a fantastic procession surges through the streets, and the night is ablaze with lights. Each town also celebrates the moulid of its own patron saint.

Egyptians share a meal after a day of fasting during Ramadan.

Important Islamic Sites

The **Blue Mosque (Mosque of Aqsunqur)** (Cairo) is famous for its indigo and turquoise tiles.

The **Citadel of Saladin** (Cairo) is a fortress that encloses the Military Museum, Gawhara Palace, and several mosques.

The **Mosque of Amr ibn al-As** (Cairo), built by Egypt's first Muslim conqueror in A.D. 642, is Egypt's oldest mosque.

The **Mosque of Ibn Tulun** (Cairo), built by the Tulunid prince Ahmed in 879, is Egypt's largest mosque.

Al-Azhar Mosque, built in 972, is Cairo's first Fatimid mosque. Its court is lined with marble columns and beautiful gypsum decorations.

Muhammad Ali Mosque (Cairo) (right) is also known as the Alabaster Mosque because of its alabaster-covered walls.

The **Mosque** and **Madrasa of Sultan Hassan** (Cairo), built in 1356, is a Mameluke structure with marble paneling. Sherbet once flowed from its fountain for special occasions.

Coptic Christians

Coptic Christians form the largest religious minority in Egypt. They are the remnants of Egypt's Christian community before the Arab conquest. The Egyptian government estimates that there are about two million Copts in Egypt, but the Copts themselves estimate their numbers at closer to seven million.

Copts enjoy freedom of worship in Egypt, but they may not preach their religion to others. While Copts may convert to Islam, Muslims may not convert to the Coptic Church. In some areas, Copts have been targets of brutal attacks by Muslim extremists.

Saint Mark is believed to have brought Christianity to Egypt in the first century A.D. The new faith blended well with Egyptians' ancient beliefs, such as the final judgment and the importance of the afterlife. Christianity's first monasteries were set up in the deserts of Egypt. The first Christian monk, Saint Anthony, was a Copt.

Copts have special reverence for the Holy Family—Jesus, Mary, and Joseph. Tradition holds that the Holy Family fled to Egypt to escape persecution. Coptic boys are baptized when they are forty days old, and girls are baptized at eighty days. Copts believe that the soul remains with the body for forty days after death.

The head of the Coptic Church—the Patriarch of Alexandria—oversees Coptic churches and monasteries throughout Egypt. The most famous historical churches are in Old Cairo on the ruins of the Roman Fortress of Babylon. Several fourth-century Coptic monasteries stand at Wadi Natrun in the desert northwest of Cairo.

Theodoros II, Patriarch of Alexandria, meets with leaders of the Greek Orthodox Church.

Coptic Holidays

In 2003, Coptic Christmas was made a national holiday in Egypt. It falls on January 7 every year. Before that, Egypt's Coptic Christians had to take it as a day off from work. This was the first time a Coptic Christian holiday was given official government recognition.

Other important Coptic holidays include Epiphany (January 19), Easter, Pentecost, and Coptic New Year (September 11). Copts also honor special saints with moulids.

Important Christian Sites

The **Cathedral of Saint Mark** (Abbassia) is the largest cathedral in Africa and supposedly contains the remains of Saint Mark the Evangelist.

The **Church of Saint Mercurius** (Cairo) contains Coptic art, including 175 icons of Old and New Testament scenes.

The **Church of Saint Sergius** was built in the early 400s and is considered Cairo's oldest church.

The **Church of the Virgin** (Cairo) displays rare icons. Its wooden aisles are inlaid with ivory.

The **Church of the Virgin** (Zaytoun) is famous because people have claimed to see the Virgin Mary above one of its domes.

The **"Hanging Church,"** built on top of the southern gate of Old Cairo's Fortress of Babylon, has three altars, a marble pulpit and pillars, and magnificent icons.

The **Monastery of Saint Anthony**, near the Red Sea coast south of Suez, is dedicated to the early Christian hermit who lived and died there. Its library houses more than 1,500 books, most in manuscript form.

The **Monastery of Saint Catherine** (below), at the foot of Mount Sinai, is a Greek Orthodox complex dating from the sixth century. Its collections include several thousand manuscripts and icons, as well as many precious gold and jeweled objects.

On July 14, they gather at the White Monastery near Sohag for Saint Shenute's moulid. Sham an-Nessim, which means "sniffing the breeze," is the day people throw open their windows and take a deep breath. This springtime "fresh air" holiday is believed to have begun in the time of the pharaohs. It falls on the Monday after Coptic Easter. Families enjoy picnics and eat salted fish, onions, and colored eggs that day.

The Ben Ezra Synagogue underwent recent restoration and is a frequent stop for tourists visiting Cairo.

Other Religious Groups

About one million Egyptians belong to other Christian groups. These include the Roman Catholic, Anglican, and Greek Orthodox churches.

A large Jewish community once flourished in Egypt. Jewish scholars translated many works of science and philosophy into Greek. They also translated the Bible's Old Testament from Hebrew into Greek. From this version, translations were made into Coptic and Latin. Today, fewer than a thousand Jews live in Egypt. The twelfth-century Ben Ezra Synagogue, in Old Cairo, is no longer used for worship.

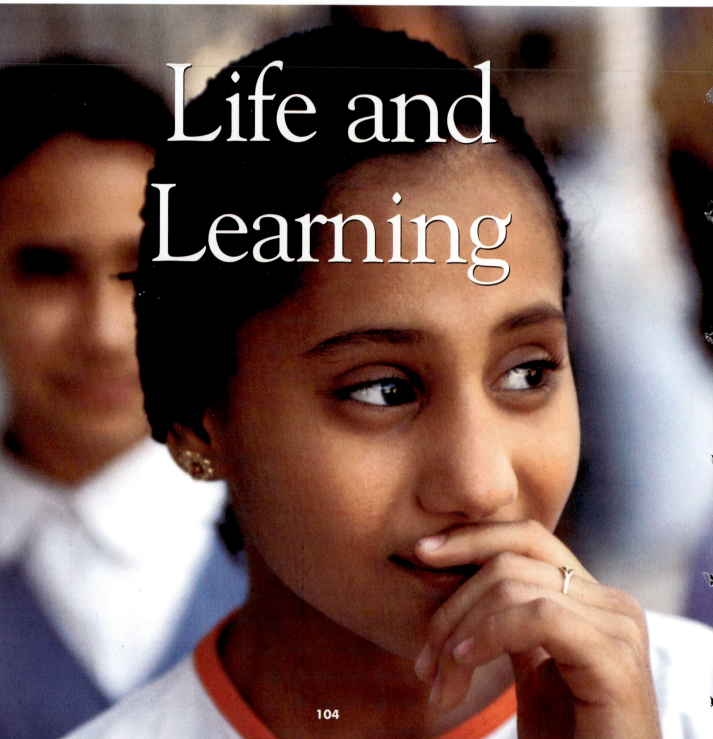

Life and Learning

Wares of all kinds can be found in the Khan al-Khalili market.

STAND BLINDFOLDED IN THE BUSTLING STREETS OF KHAN al-Khalili, and your nose will tell you where you are. Roses, cinnamon, and dozens of other sweet and savory smells fill the air. Merchants in this Cairo bazaar are famous for their exotic perfumes and spices. Other craftspeople sell handblown glass, handwoven textiles, gold jewelry, and leather goods such as camel saddles. There are carved wooden boxes and trays inlaid with mother-of-pearl; brass and copper vases, cups, and trays; and statues made of alabaster, a cloudy white stone. Egypt's cotton fabrics are known for their beautiful colors and designs.

Opposite: **A girl attends class in the Maadi area of Cairo.**

The Egyptian Museum

The Egyptian Museum in Cairo highlights five thousand years of Egyptian history. Its vast collection includes treasures from Tutankhamun's tomb. In a special room of royal mummies, the preserved bodies of ancient pharaohs are displayed in glass cases. Other displays include statues, jewelry, games, and furniture.

Down the highway south of Cairo, children are busy with needles and looms. They are learning to make traditional wall hangings and carpets at Wissa Wassef Art School in the village of Harrounia. Their work is known around the world for its bold colors and playful designs.

Music and Performing Arts

Traditional Arab instruments include the flute, oboe, viol, zither, and lute, as well as drums and tambourines. Popular songs tell tales of heartbreak and woe. Cairo's Opera House, on Gezira Island at the end of El-Tahrir Bridge, presents music and dance by Arab artists. The Orchestra for Arabic Music often performs there.

Musicians play traditional Egyptian instruments.

Umm Kulthum was Egypt's most beloved singer. More than three million grief-stricken fans joined her funeral procession in 1975. Today, Umm Kulthum Theater in Cairo hosts folk dances and other musical shows.

Belly dancing is popular in much of the Middle East. While the most conservative Muslims frown on belly dancing, others see it as a fine art. In Egypt, belly dancers perform in hotels and nightclubs.

Belly dancing is performed throughout the world, but many consider Egypt the origin of this popular form of dance.

The novels of Naguib Mahfouz have been translated into twenty-eight languages. No other Arab writer has been as widely translated.

Literature and Film

Novelist Naguib Mahfouz (1911–), Egypt's greatest modern writer, has been called the inventor of the Arabic novel. His stories of Egyptian life earned him the 1988 Nobel Prize in Literature, the world's highest literary honor. He was the first Arab writer to win the Nobel Prize. In 1994, Islamic extremists tried to kill Mahfouz. They were protesting his use of God as a character in his novel *The Children of Gebelawi*. Mahfouz is most famous for his Cairo Trilogy, which follows the story of one family from World War I to the 1950s.

Abbas al-Aqqad (1889–1964) is considered the greatest modern Arab poet. Even when he was imprisoned for political offenses, he continued to write deeply moving poetry.

Other Egyptian writers have also made their mark. Taha Hussein (1889–1973), the minister of education from 1950 to 1952, was honored for his intellectual essays. Mahmoud Taymur (1894–1973) satirized Egyptian society in popular plays. Through essays and poems, Malak Hifni Hasif (1886–1918) tried to raise the status of Egyptian women.

The first Egyptian film was *The Civil Servant*, made in 1922. Since then, Egypt has produced every kind of film, from musical comedy to serious drama. Censorship has been severe at times, but it is more relaxed now. Today, Youssef Chahine and Mohamad Khan are two of Egypt's outstanding film directors.

Education

About 58 percent of Egypt's adults can read and write—68 percent of men and 47 percent of women. Free public education is offered from primary grades through university level. Children must attend school from ages six through fourteen.

Primary schools cover ages six through eleven. Secondary schools last for six years, broken into two three-year cycles. About 93 percent of Egyptian children enroll in primary school, but about one-quarter of these students drop out after six years. The government has had great success with making schools friendlier to girls. Many more girls are going to school now and staying till they graduate.

Schoolchildren in Cairo leave school after a full day of classes.

Graduates of Egyptian universities are well prepared for professional life. The nation has thirteen major universities and dozens of technical institutes and teachers' colleges. More than 155,000 students are enrolled in Cairo University. Alexandria University is another important institution. Egypt's oldest university is the thousand-year-old Al-Azhar University in Cairo. It is a major center of learning for the Islamic world.

Students attend a lecture at Cairo University.

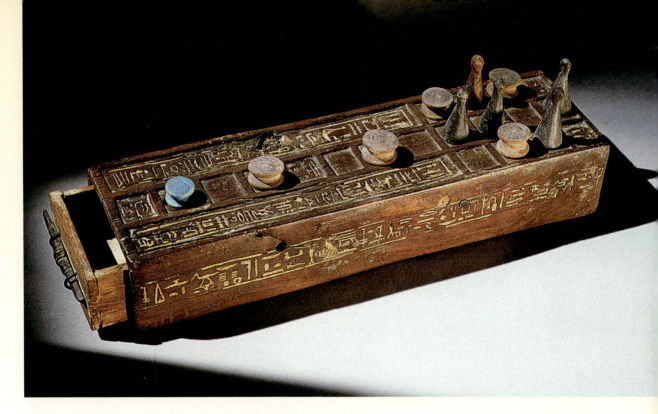

Ancient Board Games

Ancient Egyptians enjoyed playing board games. Variations of these games are still being played today. One game was senet, similar to today's game of backgammon. The game board had three rows of ten holes each. The playing pieces were sticks or bones.

Mancala boards have been found carved into the rooftops of ancient Egypt's temples. Mancala might be the oldest board game in the world. Egyptians were playing it at least as early as 1450 B.C. Today, people throughout Africa play types of mancala. The board has two rows of holes. Game pieces might be beans, nuts, or seeds. Two players move their pieces from one hole to another, trying to capture pieces. Capture all your opponent's pieces, and you win!

Many of Egypt's schools are overcrowded and suffer from a lack of money, teachers, and school buildings. There is also a constant struggle between government authorities and Islamists, who want Islamic teachings to be part of every classroom subject. The government, on the other hand, wants nonreligious subjects to remain nonreligious.

The Alexandria Library Revived

Alexandria's ancient library, built around 300 B.C., was the greatest research center of ancient times. Scholars there were the first to translate the Bible's Old Testament from Hebrew into Greek and the first to discover that the planets revolve around the Sun. The library was destroyed during a war in the third century A.D.

The Egyptian government decided to honor the early library by building a new one—the Bibliotheca Alexandrina—near the site of the original building. Kings, queens, presidents, and Nobel Prize winners from around the world attended its grand opening in 2002. The eleven-story library began with a collection of about 250,000 books, but it can hold several million. Its digital archive contains 10 billion Web pages.

Sports

Soccer is Egypt's national sport. Children play on school teams or in open fields. When professional soccer teams compete in Cairo for the annual championship, the city practically shuts down for the victory parties and parades.

Children play soccer near the Giza pyramids.

Breeding, training, and racing horses has a long tradition in Egypt. During the Mameluke period, horsemanship became a high art. Today, there are riding and racing clubs in Cairo, Alexandria, and other cities.

Graceful white sails float along the Mediterranean, the Red Sea, and the Nile. They are either standard sailboats or *feluccas*, Egypt's traditional flat-bottomed boats. Windsurfing, waterskiing, rowing, and fishing are also popular water sports.

Egyptians celebrate their long history of horsemanship at the Arabian Horse Festival in Belbies.

Rowers from around the world compete in the International Nile Rowing Competition. Egypt also hosts national and international fishing festivals every year.

The Red Sea is one of the world's best places for scuba diving and snorkeling. Its coral reefs are spectacular. Sharm el-Sheikh, on the Sinai Peninsula, is one of the finest locations. Other good diving spots are Ras Muhammad National Park, Dahab, Hurghada, and Safraga.

A scuba diver explores a vibrant coral reef in the Red Sea.

The Many
Flavors of Life

For an Egyptian villager, food is simple and hearty. Most meals include a dish made with fava beans. People boil them for hours, often overnight, to make them soft enough to eat. Sometimes beans are chopped and mixed with eggs. A ball or patty of soft beans is fried in olive oil to make *tamaiya*. In *ful*, the national dish, fava beans are mixed with various herbs and spices for flavor.

Tahina is a tasty sesame-seed paste used as a dip or sandwich spread. When chickpeas, lemon juice, and garlic are added, it become *hummus*. *Babaganoush* is another dipping paste, made with eggplants and sesame. Cubes of veal or lamb's meat are often served on a skewer as *kebabs*. *Karkadé* is made with hibiscus flowers.

Aysh, Egyptian bread, is round and flat. It puffs up to make a handy pocket for meat or vegetables. Women bake bread in clay ovens, much as their ancestors did. Egyptians often use bread instead of a spoon to scoop up food.

Opposite: **A man visits the Karnak Temple in Luxor.**

A baker carries fresh aysh through the streets of Cairo.

Getting Your Fill of Ful

Egypt's national dish—ful—is especially popular as a breakfast food. There are as many versions of ful as there are cooks. To prepare ful, cook fava beans slowly for hours until soft. Mash garlic with sea salt and add lemon juice and olive oil. Stir this mixture in with the beans, along with chopped onions and parsley. Sprinkle with paprika and other savory spices. Serve with bread wedges, spring onions, and radishes.

Milk from cows, oxen, sheep, and goats is made into cheese. In rural areas, women fill a sheepskin or a goatskin with milk. They hang the skin up by strings and gently push it back and forth. In time, heat from the sun and acids from the skin ferment the liquid, and it forms curds, or lumps of cheese.

Egyptians drink Turkish-style coffee. It is thick—almost muddy—black, and strong. People can choose to take it sweet, medium, or bitter. Tea, with sugar but no milk, is another popular drink.

A herder plays a tune while guiding a flock in the Sinai.

A Muslim woman in Alexandria wears the traditional niqab.

Traditional Clothes

To wear the veil or to not wear the veil? In Egypt, a woman's dress style is a religious concern. Islamic law requires a woman to dress modestly. For the most conservative Muslims, this means wearing the *niqab*—a long dress and veil that shows only the eyes. Many women enjoy the comfort and privacy the niqab gives them in public. At home, among family and close friends, they may wear casual or even trendy clothes.

Less conservative women wear the *hijab*. It covers the body and the hair, but leaves the face uncovered. The hijab is popular because it honors Islamic law while making it easier to perform daily activities. Female doctors, professors, and engineers, as well as housewives, are seen wearing both styles of dress.

Many Egyptian men wear the galabiyya.

Many women consider themselves good Muslims, yet choose to dress in Western clothes. Some young women start out wearing Western clothes, then switch to the veil when they are older.

The traditional dress for Egyptian men is the *galabiyya*—a full-length, loose-fitting robe. Villagers wear the *baladi* style, with a rounded neck and wide sleeves. Saudi-style robes are buttoned up to the neck. They fit more closely and the sleeves have cuffs. The *efrangi* style has a collar and cuffs like those on Western dress shirts. Many men wear a traditional Arabic checked scarf wrapped around the head. Some wear the typical Islamic skullcap, called a *kufi*.

The Garbage People

Cairo's Mokattam neighborhood is a "garbage village" of about twenty thousand people. They are the *zabbaleen*, or garbage people. Garbage is everywhere in Mokattam—in the streets, on the rooftops, and against the houses. In some places, it's piled three stories high.

Every morning, the residents of Mokattam go out into Cairo's busy streets. Using trucks or donkey carts, they collect garbage from homes, businesses, and streets. They gather about 3,000 tons (2,700 metric tons) every day. It's estimated that the zabbaleen handle about one-third of the city's garbage. With each ton of garbage, they create seven to eight jobs for themselves.

When they get back to Mokattam, the sorting begins. Women and girls sort the garbage into plastic, paper, glass, metal, and cloth. They weave the cloth into rugs, doormats, and quilts. Men and boys operate crushing and grinding machines. Almost everything is recycled and made into marketable goods or sold to factories. With their profits, the zabbaleen build new homes, educate their children, and improve their community.

The zabbaleen have received international praise for their achievements, but their way of life may be coming to an end. The government has begun hiring private companies to collect and recycle garbage.

Housing: Bursting at the Seams

In Cairo and Alexandria, most people live in apartment buildings. Apartments range from palace-like to closet-size. Most are rented, although some are owned by the people who live there. In some new complexes in Cairo, apartments cost up to several million dollars. In fancier suburbs, single-family houses may have marble floors with hot-water pipes beneath the floors for warmth. But most Egyptians do not live in such nice surroundings.

Cairo does not have enough housing for its growing population. People live and sleep wherever they can—on rooftops, in garbage dumps, or on boats. Parents, grandparents, and children often live in tiny, two- or three-room apartments. "If you fainted," some like to say, "you would not fall down."

Egypt's Nonreligious National Holidays

New Year's Day	January 1
Sinai Liberation Day	April 25
Labor Day	May 1
Evacuation Day	June 18
Revolution Day	July 23
Armed Forces Day	October 6
Suez Day	October 24
Victory Day	December 23

Some people have even set up homes in cemeteries. A district of sultans' tombs on the east edge of Cairo is known as the City of the Dead. More than one hundred thousand people live there. Residents have their own schools, shops, and mosques. Even some middle-class people live in the City of the Dead. They find it quieter and less crowded than the city center.

The fellahin live in one-story houses with flat roofs made of straw or palm wood. The thick walls are made of mud or sun-baked mud bricks. In hot weather, the roof is a cool place to sleep.

Many houses have dirt floors and no electricity or running water. People sit on mats or benches around a low table.

Some of Cairo's cemeteries have become thriving neighborhoods for the living.

Women at the Dakhla oasis sort through recently harvested hibiscus flowers.

Some people paint their houses with blue trim to ward off evil. Those who have made a pilgrimage to Mecca paint scenes from their trip on the outside walls.

Village Life

Most of the fellahin are farmers. They live in small villages along the Nile, just as their ancestors did thousands of years ago. Some own their land, while others rent land or work for landowners.

Villagers eat breakfast at about 6 A.M. before starting to work. Boys take the sheep and goats out to graze. When they are older, their fathers teach them traditional farming methods. Women bake bread in outdoor ovens. Girls milk goats, feed chickens, and fetch water from the village well, balancing baskets, water jars, or stacks of bread on their heads. The workday ends at sundown, and everyone gathers for the evening meal of rice, vegetables, and ful.

The people of Cairo do much of their shopping at the city's lively street markets.

City Life

A young boy sells magazines that he has fished out of a garbage bin. His father shines shoes, and his mother sells bread. Many thousands of people in Cairo are unemployed. Those who work may be executives, clerks, factory workers, shopkeepers, or street merchants. Child labor is illegal, but many children work long hours to help their families survive.

Almost half of all Egyptians live in urban areas. Villagers who can no longer survive on farms pour into the cities every day. Many bring their goats and chickens along. The first surprise they get is air pollution. Cairo's levels of dust and lead

Baksheesh

are among the highest in the world. Cairo's public buses are packed, and traffic is thick and wild. Drivers are aggressive and seem to make up their own rules.

Those who can afford it leave Cairo on weekends and in the hot summer months. Many go to Alexandria or to other Mediterranean cities, where they enjoy cool sea breezes, cleaner air, less noise, and more room.

In the cities, people eat breakfast around 7:30 A.M. Lunch is in mid-afternoon, and dinner is served at 10 P.M. or later. Many shops and businesses close for a two- or three-hour mid-day break. For Muslims, Friday is the holy day of the week, and many businesses close or have shorter hours on this day.

Egyptian men enjoy getting together in cafés to drink Turkish coffee, play backgammon, and smoke water pipes. People from all walks of life like to relax in outdoor cafés, where they can sit back and watch the vibrant life of the city around them.

Sidewalk vendors sell live chickens, papyrus paintings, and sweets. Cars and bicycles swerve around long-robed men guiding donkey carts. Women scurry through the maze, balancing jars or platters on their heads. Even in narrow alleys, people seem to follow unspoken "rules of the road." They know that if they give an inch here and there, everyone gets what they need.

Timeline

Egypt's History		World History	
King Menes founds the kingdom of Egypt by unifying Upper and Lower Egypt.	ca. 3100 B.C.		
Pharaohs build the Pyramids and the Great Sphinx in Giza.	ca. 2500 B.C.	2500 B.C.	Egyptians build the Pyramids and the Sphinx in Giza.
King Tutankhamun reigns.	ca. 1300s B.C.		
		563 B.C.	The Buddha is born in India.
The Persians conquer Egypt.	525 B.C.		
Alexander the Great takes over Egypt and founds Alexandria.	332 B.C.		
Egypt becomes part of the Roman Empire.	30 B.C.		
		A.D. 313	The Roman emperor Constantine recognizes Christianity.
Muslim Arab armies conquer Egypt.	A.D. 642	610	The Prophet Muhammad begins preaching a new religion called Islam.
The Fatimid dynasty rules Egypt.	969–1171	1054	The Eastern (Orthodox) and Western (Roman) Catholic Churches break apart.
		1066	William the Conqueror defeats the English in the Battle of Hastings.
Saladin becomes sultan of Egypt.	1171	1095	Pope Urban II proclaims the First Crusade.
The Mamelukes take control of Egypt.	1250	1215	King John seals the Magna Carta.
		1300s	The Renaissance begins in Italy.
The Pharos of Alexandria is destroyed in an earthquake.	1375	1347	The Black Death sweeps through Europe.
		1453	Ottoman Turks capture Constantinople, conquering the Byzantine Empire.
		1492	Columbus arrives in North America.
Ottoman Turks invade Egypt and rule for almost 300 years.	1517	1500s	The Reformation leads to the birth of Protestantism.
		1776	The Declaration of Independence is signed.

Egypt's History

Napoleon Bonaparte invades Egypt.	1798
The Rosetta Stone is discovered.	1799
The Suez Canal is completed.	1869
Britain declares Egypt a protectorate.	1914
Britain grants Egypt limited independence; Fu'ad I becomes king.	1922
The Muslim Brotherhood is founded.	1928
Army officers led by Gamal Abdel Nasser overthrow King Farouk.	1952
Egypt is declared a republic.	1953
Egypt seizes control of the Suez Canal.	1956
Israel occupies the Sinai and Gaza in the Six-Day War.	1967
The Aswan High Dam is completed.	1970
Egypt and Israel clash in the October War.	1973
Egypt's Anwar Sadat and Israel's Menachem Begin sign the Camp David Accords.	1978
Anwar Sadat is assassinated; Hosni Mubarak becomes president.	1981
Fifty-eight tourists are killed near Luxor, allegedly by an Islamic group.	1997
A constitutional amendment allows multiple candidates to run for president; terrorist bombers attack in Cairo and Sharm el-Sheikh.	2005

World History

1789	The French Revolution begins.
1865	The American Civil War ends.
1914	World War I breaks out.
1917	The Bolshevik Revolution brings communism to Russia.
1929	Worldwide economic depression begins.
1939	World War II begins, following the German invasion of Poland.
1945	World War II ends.
1957	The Vietnam War starts.
1969	Humans land on the moon.
1975	The Vietnam War ends.
1979	Soviet Union invades Afghanistan.
1983	Drought and famine in Africa.
1989	The Berlin Wall is torn down as communism crumbles in Eastern Europe.
1991	Soviet Union breaks into separate states.
1992	Bill Clinton is elected U.S. president.
2000	George W. Bush is elected U.S. president.
2001	Terrorists attack World Trade Center, New York, and the Pentagon, Washington, D.C.

Fast Facts

Official name:	Arab Republic of Egypt
Capital:	Cairo
Official language:	Arabic
Official religion:	Islam

Cairo

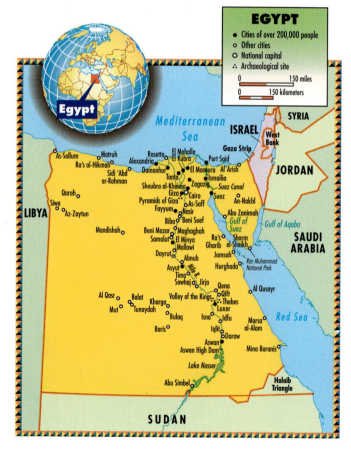

Egypt's flag

Farafra oasis

Year of founding: Menes, the first pharaoh, united Egypt in about 3100 B.C. In 1922, Egypt became an independent nation. In 1953, Egypt became a republic.

Founder: Gamal Abdel Nasser is considered the father of the Egyptian republic.

National anthem: "Biladi" ("My Homeland")

Government: Republic

Head of state: President

Head of government: Prime minister

Area: 386,900 square miles (1,002,071 sq km)

Greatest distance, north to south: 675 miles (1,086 km)

Greatest distance, east to west: 780 miles (1,255 km)

Borders: The Mediterranean Sea to the north; the Gaza Strip, Israel, and the Red Sea to the east; Sudan to the south; and Libya to the west

Highest elevation: Jabal Katrina (Mount Saint Catherine), 8,652 feet (2,637 m)

Lowest elevation: In the Qattara Depression, 436 feet (133 m) below sea level

Average temperatures: Alexandria, 59°F (15°C) in January, 79°F (26°C) in July
Aswan, 62°F (17°C) in January, 93°F (34°C) in July

Average annual rainfall: Alexandria, 7 inches (18 cm); Aswan, 0.1 inch (.25 cm)

The Sphinx

National population (2005 est.): 77,505,756

Population of largest cities (2005 est):

Cairo	7,438,376
Alexandria	3,693,412
Giza	2,541,837
Shoubra al-Kheima	1,021,862
Port Said	533,299
Suez	508,350

Famous landmarks:
- ▶ *Aswan High Dam and Lake Nasser*, Aswan
- ▶ *Great Pyramid and Sphinx*, Giza
- ▶ *Hatshepsut's Mortuary Temple*, Deir el-Bahri
- ▶ *Step pyramid of Djoser*, Saqqara
- ▶ *Temple of Amun*, Karnak
- ▶ *Temple of Luxor and Avenue of the Sphinxes*, Luxor
- ▶ *Temple of Ramses II*, Abu Simbel
- ▶ *Valley of the Kings and Valley of the Queens*, across the Nile from Luxor

Industry: Food processing is the largest manufacturing industry in Egypt. Cottonseed oil, refined sugar, meat, and milk are among the leading food products. Petroleum refining is another major industry. Cotton and wool textiles are important manufactures. Other products include fertilizers, rubber tires, cement, automobiles, and other metal goods. Petroleum and natural gas are the top mining products.

Currency

Currency: The Egyptian pound. In April 2006, one U.S. dollar equaled 5.75 Egyptian pounds.

System of weights and measures: Metric system

Egyptian children

Literacy rate:	58%	
Common Arabic words and phrases:	*Assalaamu aleikum*	Hello
	Aywa	Yes
	Bekaam?	How much?
	Feyn . . . ?	Where is . . . ?
	La	No
	Ma salaama	Good-bye
	Minfadlik	Please (to a woman)
	Minfadlak	Please (to a man)
	Shukran	Thank you

Famous Egyptians:	Abbas al-Aqqad	(1889–1964)
	Poet, novelist, and essayist	
	Farouk	(1920–1965)
	Last king of Egypt, 1936–1952	
	Hatshepsut	(1500s–1400s B.C.)
	Female pharaoh	
	Khufu	(ca. 2572–ca. 2465 B.C.)
	Builder of the Great Pyramid	
	Umm Kulthum	(1904–1975)
	Popular singer	
	Naguib Mahfouz	(1911–)
	Novelist, Nobel Prize winner	
	Menes	(ca. 3100 B.C.)
	Unifier of Upper and Lower Egypt	
	Hosni Mubarak	(1928–)
	President, 1981–	
	Muhammad Ali	(1769–1849)
	The father of modern Egypt; ruled 1805–1849	
	Gamal Abdel Nasser	(1918–1970)
	President, 1954–1970	
	Ramses II	(1200s B.C.)
	Builder of many colossal statues	
	Anwar Sadat	(1918–1981)
	President, 1970–1981	

Naguib Mahfouz

To Find Out More

Nonfiction

▶ Barghusen, Joan D., and Bob Moulder (illustrator). *Daily Life in Ancient and Modern Cairo*. Minneapolis, Minn.: Runestone Press, 2001.

▶ Bowden, Rob. *Settlements of the River Nile*. Chicago: Heinemann, 2005.

▶ Giblin, James Cross, and Bagram Ibatoulline (illustrator). *Secrets of the Sphinx*. New York: Scholastic, 2004.

▶ Hart, George. *Ancient Egypt*. New York: DK Children, 2004.

▶ Johnson, Darv. *The Longest River*. San Diego: KidHaven Press, 2003.

▶ Kaplan, Sarah Pitt. *The Great Pyramid at Giza: Tomb of Wonders*. Danbury, Conn.: Children's Press, 2005.

▶ Nicolotti, Muriel. *Madhi: A Child of Egypt*. Farmington Hills, Mich.: Blackbirch, 2005.

▶ Pateman, Robert, and Salwa El-Hamamsy. *Egypt*. New York: Benchmark, 2004.

▶ Shuter, Jane. *Life in an Egyptian Workers' Village*. Chicago: Heinemann, 2005.

▶ Winters, Kay, and Barry Moser (illustrator). *Voices of Ancient Egypt*. Washington, D.C.: National Geographic Children's, 2003.

Fiction

▶ Henty, George A. *The Cat of Bubastes: A Tale of Ancient Egypt*. Mineola, N.Y.: Dover, 2002.

▶ Sands, Emily, and Ian Andrew, Nick Harris, and Helen Ward (illustrators). *Egyptology*. Cambridge, Mass.: Candlewick, 2004.

▶ Turner, Ann Warren. *Maia of Thebes*. New York: Scholastic, 2005.

Videos & DVDs

▶ *Discovering Egypt.* 120 minutes. Questar, 2001.

▶ *Egypt: Beyond the Pyramids.* 200 minutes. A&E Home Video, 2001.

▶ *Egypt Eternal: The Quest for Lost Tombs.* 60 minutes. National Geographic, 2002.

▶ *Exotic Egypt.* 120 minutes. National Geographic, 2003.

▶ *Families of Egypt.* 30 minutes. Master Communication, 2003.

▶ *Mummies and the Wonders of Ancient Egypt.* A&E Entertainment, 2001.

▶ *Mysteries of Egypt.* 150 minutes. Kultur Video, 2001.

Web Sites

▶ **Ancient Egypt by History Link 101**
http://www.historylink101.com/ancient_egypt.htm
To find out about ancient Egyptian art, medicine, games, farming, and much more.

▶ **Ancient Egypt Webquest**
http://www.iwebquest.com/egypt/ancientegypt.htm
To learn about mummies, hieroglyphics, and daily life in ancient Egypt.

▶ **Animals in Ancient Egypt**
http://www.ri.net/schools/Smithfield/Animals/task.html
To learn about various animals and their importance in ancient Egypt.

Embassies and Organizations

▶ **Egyptian Tourist Authority**
630 Fifth Avenue, Suite 2305
New York, NY 10111
212-956-6439
http://www.egypttourism.org/

▶ **Embassy of the Arab Republic of Egypt**
3521 International Court, NW
Washington, DC 20008
202-895-5400
http://www.egyptembassy.us/

Index

Page numbers in *italics*
indicate illustrations.

A

Abbasid caliphs, 53, 54
Abbassia, 102
Abu Simbel, 49
Academy of the Arabic Language, 20
administrative courts, 67
African continent, 16, 19
agama (gray lizard), 30
agriculture, 21, *74*
Aswan High Dam and, 24, 77, *77*, 78
  cattle egrets, 35
  cotton, 9, 76
  crops, 9, 76, *76*, 78, 125
  Delta region and, 21
  deserts and, 18
  fellahin (rural farmers), 89, *89*,
    124, 125
  governorates and, 68
  growing seasons, 77, 78
  harvest, 41
  irrigation, 24, *24*, 56, 75, 78
  livestock, 25, 88, 120, *120*
  methods, 10–11
  Nile River and, 15, 19, *19*, 39, 76
  Roman Empire and, 52
  shadoof (watersweep), 77
  silt, 41
Ahmad Hamdi road tunnel, 82
Ahmose (Theban prince), 48
airports, 75, 84

al-Ahram (the *Pyramids*) newspaper, 85
al-Ahram Weekly newspaper, 85
al-Akhbar (the *News*) newspaper, 85
Al-Azhar Mosque, 94, 96, 100
Al-Azhar University, 54, 112
al-Jumhuriyah (the *Republic*)
    newspaper, 85
Alabaster Mosque. *See* Muhammad
    Ali Mosque.
Alexander the Great, 20, 50
Alexandria, 17, 20, 21, 50, 51, 52, 54,
    68, 84, 87, *87*, 88, 114, 123
Alexandria University, 112
Ali, Muhammad, 57, 58, 133
Amenhotep III (pharaoh), 20
Amun (Egyptian god), 43, *43*
Anglican Church, 103
animal life. *See also* marine life;
    reptilian life.
  birds, 34–35, *34*, *35*, 37
  camels, 14, 27, 33, *33*, 45, 88
  deserts, 30–31, 32–33
  fennecs, 30, *30*
  horses, 116, *116*
  ibex, 31, *31*
  livestock, 25, 88, 120, *120*
  Nile River valley, 29
  pyramids, 29
  Ras Muhammad National
    Park, 37
  rodents, 31, 32
  temples, 29
  wild cats, 32–33
Anthony (saint), 101
Antony, Mark, 51, 52
Anubis (Egyptian god), 44
al-Aqqad, Abbas, 109
Arab Gas Pipeline, 81
Arabian Horse Festival, *116*
Arabic language, 12, 53, 58, 82, 85,
    91–93, *92*
Arabic numerals, 93

archaeology, 20, 51, 58
art, 12, 54
al-As, Amr ibn, 53
al-Asafirah district, 87
Asian continent, 16
Aswan, 8, 17, 27, 46, 81, 84
Aswan High Dam, 23–24, 60, 77, *77*,
    78, 91
Augustus (emperor of Rome), 51, 52
Avenue of the Sphinxes, 20
aysh (food), 119, *119*
Ayyubid dynasty, 55

B

babaganoush (food), 119
Bahariya oasis, 22
baksheesh (money for the
    poor), 127
baladi style (clothing), 122
Baris oasis, 22
Bastet (Egyptian goddess), 33
Battle of el-Alamein, 59, *59*
Battle of the Pyramids, 56
Baybars (Mameluke general), 55
bazaars, 105
Bedouins, 25, 27, 88, 89, 90
Begin, Menachem, 61, *61*
belly dancing, 108, *108*
Ben Ezra Synagogue, 103, *103*
Bibliotheca Alexandrina, 20, *114*,
    114
"Biladi" (national anthem), 69
birds, 34–35, *34*, *35*, 37
Blue Mosque. *See* Mosque of
    Aqsunqur.
Blue Nile, 19
board games, 113, *113*
Bonaparte, Napoleon, 56, 57
Book of the Dead, 44
borders, 17, 23
burial chambers. *See* tombs.
Byzantine Empire, 53

C

Caesar, Julius, 51
Cairo, *14*, 19, 45, 54, 56, 62, 64, 68, 72–73, *72*, *73*, 82, *82*, 83, 84, 85, 86, 87, 88, 94, *95*, 98, 99, 100, 102, *104*, 105, 106, *106*, 108, *111*, 112, *119*, 123, 124, 126–127, *126*
Cairo Tower, 72
Cairo Trilogy (Naguib Mahfouz), 109
Cairo University, 20, 112, *112*
caliphs, 53, 54, 56
Cambyses (Persian prince), 49
camels, *14*, *27*, 33, *33*, 45, 88
Camp David Accords, 61
canals, 16, 20, 56, 58, 59, 60, 78, 83, 84, *84*, 87
caracals (desert lynx), 33
Carnarvon, Lord, 58
Carter, Howard, 58
Carter, Jimmy, 61
Cathedral of Saint Mark, 102
cattle egrets, 35
censorship, 110
ceramics, 41, *41*, 55
Chahine, Youssef, 110, *110*
Champollion, Jean-François, 57
The Children of Gebelawi (Naguib Mahfouz), 109
children, 9–10, *9*, 89, *104*, 107, *111*, 111, 125, 126
Christianity, 52, 54, 69, 93, 96, 101, 102, 103
Church of Saint Mercurius, 102
Church of Saint Sergius, 102
Church of the Virgin, 102
Citadel of Saladin, 73, 98, 100
cities. *See also* towns; villages.
　air pollution in, 126–127
　Alexandria, 17, 20, 21, 50, 51, 52, 54, 68, 84, 87, *87*, 88, 114, 123
　Cairo, *14*, 19, 45, 54, 56, 62, 64,

68, 72–73, *72*, *73*, 82, *82*, 83, 84, *85*, 86, 87, 88, 94, *95*, 98, 99, 100, 102, *104*, 105, 106, *106*, 108, *111*, 112, *119*, 123, 124, 126–127, 126
al-Fustat (Old Cairo), 53, 73, 101, 102, 103
Giza, 20, 81, 88
Harrounia, 107
Heliopolis, 84
Hurghada, 18, *18*, 81, 84
Ismailia, 68
Luxor, 20, 28, 58, 62, 76, 81, 84, *118*
Memphis, 47, 50
Port Said, 20, 68, 81, 84, 88
Sharm el-Sheikh, 26, *26*, 84
Shoubra al-Kheima suburb, 20, 88
Suez, 20, 68, 84, 88
Thebes, 20, 33, 47, 48
Zaytoun, 102
cities of the dead, 49
City of the Dead, 124, *124*
The Civil Servant (film), 110
Cleopatra (pharaoh), 51, *51*, 52
Cleopatra's Needles, 20
climate, 17, 19, 27, 46
clothing, 70, 90, 121–122, *121*, *122*
coastline, 17, 18, *18*, 24, 35, 75, 80, 81, 88
Colored Canyon, 25
communications, 85, *85*
Constantine (emperor of Rome), 52
Coptic Church, 52, 73, 89–90, 93, *93*, 100, 101, 102
Coptic language, 53, 93
Coptic Museum, 73
coral reefs, 36, *36*, 37, 117, *117*
cotton, 9, 76
court of cassation, 67–68
courts of general jurisdiction, 67
crafts, 105, 107
crest of Saladin, 68

Crusades, 54, 55, 55
currency (Egyptian pound), 79, *79*

D

Dakhla oasis, 22, *24*, 125
Damietta, 84
dance, 107, 108, *108*
Darwish, Sayed, 69
date palms, 37, *37*, 76
Deir el-Bahri, 49
Delta region, 19, 21, 24, 32, 37, 39, 76
demotic writing, 57, 93
desert foxes. *See* fennecs.
desert lynx. *See* caracals.
deserts, *14*, 15, 16–18, *16*, 21–22, *23*, 27, 30, 75, 78, 81, 85, 87
Diocletian (emperor of Rome), 52
Djoser (pharaoh), 45

E

Eastern Desert, 16, 18
economy
　agriculture, 76, 78
　foreign trade, 41, 54, 55, 61, 75, 79, 80, 84
　inflation, 75
　manufacturing, 57, 78, 79, *79*
　marketplaces, *12*, *105*, *126*, 127
　mining, 78, 80–81, *80*
　privatization, 62, 75
　tourism, 18, 25, 26, 45, 81
　unemployment, 75
education, 9–10, *10*, 11, 12, 57–58, 68, *104*, 107, 111–113, *111*, *112*
eels, 36, 37
efrangi style (clothing), 122
egrets, *35*
Egyptian Gazette newspaper, 85
Egyptian Museum, 72, 106, *106*
Egyptian pound (currency), 79, *79*
Egyptian Radio and Television Union (ERTU), 85

Egyptian wild cats. *See* Kaffir cats.
El-Mugamma building, 64
Empereur, Jean-Yves, 51
English language, 82, 85, 91, *92*
executive branch of government,
   65–66, 67

F

Farafra oasis, *21*, 22
Farouk (king of Egypt), 60
Fatimid dynasty, 54, 73
fava beans, 119, 120
Fayyum settlement, 22, 37
fellahin (rural farmers), 89, *89*,
   124, 125
feluccas (boats), 116
fennecs (desert foxes), 30, *30*
festivals, 12, 98–99, *116*, 117
fishing, 26, 80, 116, 117
Five Pillars of Faith, 97
flamingoes, 34
flooding, 19, *19*, 41, 46, 78
food, 12, *12*, 119–120, *119*, 127
forests, 37
Fortress of Babylon, 73, 101, 102
France, 56, 57, 58
French language, 91, 92
Fu'ad I (king of Egypt), 59
ful (national dish), 119, 120, 125
al-Fustat (Old Cairo), 53, 73, 101,
   102, 103

G

galabiyya (clothing), 122, *122*
games, 106, 113, *113*
garbage villages, 123
geography
   borders, 17, 23
   Delta region, 19, 21, 24, 32, 37,
      39, 76
   deserts, *14*, 15, 16–18, *16*, 21–22,
      23, 27, 30, 75, 78, 81, 85, 87

elevation, 17
Jabal Katrina (Mount Saint
   Catherine), 17, 25
Jabal Musa (Mount Sinai), 25, *25*
Qattara Depression, 17, 18
wadis (ravines), 18, 35, 101
geopolitical map, *11*
Germany, 59
Gezira Island, 72, 107
Giza, 20, 81, 88
government. *See also* local government.
   administrative courts, 67
   constitution, 65, 66, 68
   court of cassation, 67–68
   courts of general jurisdiction, 67
   education and, 12
   El-Mugamma building, *64*
   elections, 65, 66
   executive branch, 65–66, 67
   independence, 58, 59
   Islam and, 68–70
   judicial branch, 65, 67–68
   legislative branch, 65, 66–67, *66*
   military, 47, 48, 53, 57, 60, 65–66
   muhafazat (governorates), 68
   People's Assembly, 65, 66–67, *66*,
      70, 71
   "political Islam" movement, 69–70
   political parties, 70–71
   presidents, 23, 60, 61, *61*, 62, 65,
      66, 67, *70*
   scribes, 40
   Shari'a (Islamic code of law),
      68–69
   Supreme Constitutional Court, 67
   voting rights, 65, 66
Great Britain, 56, 57, 58, 60, 85
Great Pyramid at Giza, 20, 45, *45*, 46,
   73, *74*, *81*, 115
Great Sphinx, 20, 45, 46, *46*, 81
Greco-Roman Museum, 20

Greek Empire, 20, 50
Greek Orthodox Church, *101*, 102, 103
Gulf of Aqaba, 17, 26, 60–61
Gulf of Suez, 20, 26, 58, 80, 81

H

"Hanging Church," 102
Harrounia, 107
Hasif, Malak Hifni, 110
Hatshepsut (pharaoh), 49, *49*
Heliopolis, 84
Herodotus (Greek historian), 13, 46
herons, 34, *34*
hieroglyphs, 42, *42*, 47, 57
hijab (clothing), 121
historical maps. *See also* maps.
   Ancient Egypt, *47*
   Greek and Roman Egypt, *52*
   Napoleon's Invasion of Egypt, *56*
holidays
   national, 124
   religious, 98–99, 102–103
horsemanship, 116
horses, 116, *116*
hummus (food), 119
Hurghada, 18, *18*, 81, 84
Hussein, Saddam, 62
Hussein, Taha, 110
hydroelectric power, 24
Hyksos people, 47, 48

I

ibex (mountain goats), 31, *31*
ibis (birds), 35
'Id al-Adha festival, 99
'Id al-Fitr feast, 99
iftar (fast-breaking feast), 98
Imhotep (architect), 45
insect life, 30, 35, *35*
Inshallah ("God willing"), 98
International Nile Rowing
   Competition, 117

Iraq, 48, 53, 62, 63
irrigation, 24, 24, 37, 56, 75, 78
Islamic calendar, 97
Islamic religion, 12, 53, 63, 68–70,
    71, 88, 95, 95, 100, 113, 121, 127
Ismailia, 68
Israel, 17, 59, 60–61, 62, 71, 90
Italy, 54, 59, 83

J

Jabal Katrina (Mount Saint
    Catherine), 17, 25
Jabal Musa (Mount Sinai), 25, 25
Jawhar (Fatimid general), 54
Jerusalem, 54, 55
jewelry, 35, 40, 40, 105, 106
al-Jihad (Holy Struggle)
    fundamentaist group, 62, 71
Jordan, 61, 81, 83, 90
Judaism, 59, 69, 103
judicial branch of government, 65,
    67–68

K

Kaffir cats, 32
karkadé (food), 119
Karnak, 20, 43, 47, 49, 81
kebabs (food), 119
khamsin (wind), 27
Khan al-Khalili souq, 72–73, 105, 105
Khan, Mohamad, 110
Kharga oasis, 22
Khepri (Egyptian god), 35
Khufu (pharaoh), 45, 46
kohl (eyeliner), 40
kufi (skullcap), 122
Kulthum, Umm, 108

L

Lake Nasser, 17, 23, 23, 24, 35, 91
languages, 12, 53, 58, 82, 85, 91–93, 92

legislative branch of government, 65,
    66–67, 66
Library of Alexandria, 20
Libyan Desert. *See* Western Desert.
literature, 54, 109–110, 109
livestock, 25, 88, 120, 120
local government, 68. *See also*
    government.
lotus plants, 37
Lower Egypt, 15, 39
Lower Nile, 15
Luxor, 20, 28, 58, 62, 76, 81, 84, 118

M

madrasas (religious schools), 73
Mahfouz, Naguib, 109, 109
makeup, 40
Mamelukes (soldier-bodyguards), 55,
    56, 100, 116
mancala (board game), 113
mangrove trees, 37
manufacturing, 57, 78, 79, 79
maps. *See also* historical maps.
    Cairo, 73
    geopolitical, 11
    natural resources, 81
    population density, 88
    topographic, 17
marine life, 18, 34, 35, 36, 36, 37, 80
Mark (saint), 101, 102
marketplaces, 12, 105, 126, 127
mastabas (tombs), 45
Mediterranean coastal strip, 75
Mediterranean Sea, 17, 19, 20, 24,
    27, 50, 58, 59, 75, 84, 88, 116, 127
Memphis, 47, 50
Menes (pharaoh), 39, 47
Mentuhotep II (pharaoh), 47
Middle Kingdom, 47
minarets, 94, 96
Mokattam neighborhood, 123

Monastery of Saint Anthony, 102
Monastery of Saint Catherine,
    102, 102
Mosque and Madrasa of Sultan
    Hassan, 100
Mosque of Amr ibn al-As, 100
Mosque of Aqsunqur, 100
Mosque of Ibn Tulun, 73, 100
motion-picture industry, 20, 110, 110
Moulid an-Nabi, 99
moulids (holidays), 99, 102–103
Mount Saint Catherine.
    See Jabal Katrina.
Mount Sinai. *See* Jabal Musa.
Mubarak, Hosni, 62–63, 65–66, 70,
    70, 71
muhafazat (governorates), 68
Muhammad (Islamic prophet), 53,
    96, 98
Muhammad Ali Mosque, 73, 95,
    100, 100
al-Muizz (caliph), 54
mummification, 44
music, 12, 69, 107, 107
Muslim Brotherhood, 71
Muslims. *See* Islamic religion.

N

Nabataean people, 92
Nasser, Gamal Abdel, 23, 60, 60,
    61, 65–66
national anthem, 69
National Democratic Party (NDP),
    70, 70
national dish, 119, 120
national emblem, 68
national flag, 68, 68
national holidays, 124
National Progressive Unionist
    Party, 70
national sport, 115
natural gas, 80, 81

natural resources map, *81*
necropolis (city of the dead), 20
New Kingdom, 47, 48, 49
New Valley oases, 22, 78
New Wafd Party, 70
newspapers, 85, *85*
Nile crocodiles, 29
Nile Delta, 19, 21, 24, 32, 37, 39, 76
Nile River, 8, 15, *15*, 17, 19, *19*, 22,
    34, 37, *37*, 41, 46, 72, *72*, 78, 81,
    87, 125
Nile River Valley, 15, 24, 28, 29, 76
niqab (clothing), 121, *121*
Nubians, 89, 90, 91

O

oases, 21–22, *21*, *22*, 24, 85, 87, 125
Octavian. See Augustus.
October War, 61
oil, 75, *75*, 80–81, *80*
Old Cairo. *See* al-Fustat.
Old Kingdom, 47
Opera House/Cultural Center
    (Cairo), 72, 107
oracles, 50
Orchestra for Arabic Music, 107
Osiris (Egyptian god), 44
Ottoman Empire, 56, 58

P

Palestine, 48, 54, 55, 59
papyrus, 37, 47, 127
Pasha, Ismail, 58
Pasha, Said, 58
passenger ferries, 83
Patriarch of Alexandria, 101
people
    Bedouins, 25, *27*, 88, 89, 90
    charity, 127
    children, 9–10, *9*, 89, *104*, 107,
      111, *111*, 125, 126
    classes, 39–41

clothing, 70, 90, 121–122, *121*, *122*
education, 9–10, *10*, 11, 12,
    57–58, 68, *104*, 107, 111–113,
    111, *112*
family planning, 88
fellahin (rural farmers), 89, *89*,
    124, 125
food, 12, *12*, 119–120, *119*, 127
health care, 68
housing, 68, 123–125
Hyksos, 47, 48
jewelry, 35, 40, *40*, 105
languages, 12, 53, 58, 82, 85,
    91–93, *92*
life spans, 44
literacy, 111
makeup, 40
marriages, 11
minority groups, 89
Nabataeans, 92
Nubians, 89, 90, 91
population, 87, 88, *88*
unemployment, 126
voting rights, 65, 66
women, 12, *15*, 40, 41, 65, 66, 70,
    110, 111, 119, 120, 121–122,
    123, 125, *125*, 127
zabbaleen (garbage people), 123
People's Assembly, 65, 66–67, *66*,
    70, 71
petroleum, 78, 79, 80
pharaohs, 20, *38*, 39, 43, 45, 47, 48,
    49, *49*, 50, 51, *51*, 52, 58, 106
Pharos of Alexandria lighthouse,
    20, 51
plant life, 21, 37, *37*
"political Islam" movement, 69–70
political parties, 70–71
population density map, 88
Port Said, 20, 68, 81, 84, 88
pottery, 41, *41*, 55
Ptolemaic Period, 47, 50–52

Ptolemy (pharaoh), 50
pyramids, 13, 20, 29, 45–46, *45*, 73,
    74, 81, *115*

Q

Qattara Depression, 17, 18
Qur'an (Islamic holy book), 91, 96, 98

R

radio, 85, 91
railroads, 83
Ramadan (Muslim holy month),
    97, 98, 99, *99*
Ramses II (pharaoh), 20, 49
Ramses III (pharaoh), 49
Ras al-Sana al-Hegira festival, 99
Ras Muhammad National Park,
    37, 117
Re (Egyptian god), 33, 43
Red Sea, 17, 18, *18*, 26, *26*, 35, 36,
    36, 37, 54, *75*, 80, 81, 84, 88, 116,
    117, *117*
religion
    Anglican Church, 103
    Ben Ezra Synagogue, 103, *103*
    call to prayer, 96
    cats and, 33
    Christianity, 52, 54, 69, 93, 96,
      101, 102
    Coptic Church, 52, 73, 89–90, 93,
      93, 100, 101, 102
    Five Pillars of Faith, 97
    goddesses, 43
    gods, 43
    holidays, 98–99, 102–103
    iftar (fast-breaking feast), 98
    Inshallah ("God willing"), 98
    Islam, 12, 53, 63, 68–70, 71, 88,
      95, *95*, 97, 100, 113, 121, 127
    Islamic calendar, 97
    Judaism, 59, 69, 103

minarets, 94, 96
mosques, 73, 94, 95, 96, 96, 100, *100*
moulids, 99, 102–103
muezzin, 96
Qur'an, 91, 96, 98
Ramadan, 97, 98, 99, *99*
Roman Catholic Church, 54, 103
Shari'a (Islamic code of law), 68–69
reptilian life, 29, 30, 31
Richard the Lionheart, 55
roadways, 82
rock hyraxes, 31
Roda Island, 72
rodents, 31, 32
Roman Catholic Church, 54, 103
Roman Empire, 51, 52–53
Rosetta Stone, 57, *57*
rowing, 116–117

S

Sadat, Anwar, 61, *61*, 62, 65–66, 70
Safraga, 84, 117
Sahara Desert, 16, 23
sailing, 8, 116
Saladin (sultan), 54–55, *55*
sand boas, 31
sand cats, 32
sand foxes. *See* fennecs.
Saqqara, 45
Saudi Arabia, 90, 96, 98
saudi robes, 122
saw-scaled vipers, 31
scarabs, 35, *35*
scribes, 39–40, *39*
scuba diving, 117, *117*
Selim (sultan), 56
senet (board game), 113
Shari'a (Islamic code of law), 68–69
Sharm el-Sheikh, 26, *26*, 84
Shoubra al-Kheima suburb, 20, 88
silt, 41

Sinai Peninsula, 16, 25, 27, *27*, 37, 61, 62, 81, 88, 90, 117
Siwa oasis, 22, *22*
Six-Day War, 61
soccer, 115, *115*
sports, 115–117, *115*
St. John's Reef, *36*
statues, 49, 106
step pyramids, 45
street vendors, *12, 126,* 127
Suez, 20, 68, 84, 88
Suez Canal, 16, 58, 59, 60, 61, 82, 84, 84, 87
Supreme Constitutional Court, 67
Syria, 48, 53, 54, 55, 61

T

taxation, 41
taxes, 51, 52
Taymur, Mahmoud, 110
telephones, 85
television, 85
Temple of Abu Simbel, 23
Temple of Amun, 20, 43, 47, 49
Temple of Karnak, 81, 118
Temple of Luxor, 20
Temple of Philae, 23, 81
Temple of Ramses II, 81
Temple of Thebes, 81
temples, 13, 29, 43, 49
terrorism, 62, 71, 81
Thebes, 20, 33, 47, 48
Theodoros II (patriarch of Alexandria), *101*
Thutmose I (pharaoh), 49
Thutmose II (pharaoh), 49
Thutmose III (pharaoh), 38, 48, 49
tombs, 13, *13,* 44, 45, 48, 49, 50, 106,124
Tombs of the Nobles, 49
topographic map, *17*
tourism, *18,* 25, 26, 45, 81

transportation, *14,* 24, 33, *33,* 45, 46, 75, 82–83, *82,* 83–84, 84, 88, 127
Turkey, 53, 55, 56
Tutankhamun (pharaoh), *48,* 50, *50,* 58, 106

U

Umayyad caliphs, 53
Umm Kulthum Theater, 108
United States, 60, 61, 62, 85
University of Cairo. *See* Cairo University.
Upper Egypt, 15, 20, 27, 37, 39
Upper Nile, 15
Urban II (pope), 54

V

Valley of the Kings, 13, *13,* 20, *48,* 49, 50, 81
Valley of the Queens, 20, 49
villages, 10, 18, 26, 60, 68, 81, 89, 93, 107, 119, 122, 123, 125, 126. *See also* cities.

W

Wadi al Rayan, 35
Wadi Natrun, 101
wadis (ravines), 18
water hyacinths, 37
water sports, 116–117, *117*
Western Desert, 16, *16,* 17, 21–22, 75, 78, 81, 85
White Desert, 16
White Nile, 19
Wissa Wassef Art School, 107
World War I, 58
World War II, 59, *59*

Z

zabbaleen (garbage people), 123
Zaytoun, 102

Meet the Author

ANN HEINRICHS fell in love with faraway places as a child while reading Doctor Dolittle books and Peter Freuchen's *Book of the Seven Seas*. As an adult, she has tried to cover as much of the earth as possible. She has traveled through most of the United States and much of Europe, as well as Africa, the Middle East, and East Asia.

Ann's travels in Egypt gave her rich insights into the country's culture, history, and natural resources. She rode camels, trekked through deserts, scaled massive rock formations, climbed Mount Sinai, shopped in bazaars, and visited the pyramids and the Sphinx. Riding a camel was one of her favorite experiences. "Camels are much more comfortable than horses," she says, "and they move along with a gentle lurch that's really hypnotizing."

"Trips are fun, but my real work begins at the library. I head straight for the reference department. Some of my favorite resources are United Nations publications, *Europa World Yearbook*, and the periodicals databases. For this book, I also read English-language issues of the Egyptian newspaper *Al-Ahram* to get a feel for Egyptians' current interests and viewpoints. Talking with Egyptian people about their country and culture gave me valuable insights, too.

"For me, writing nonfiction is a bigger challenge than writing fiction. Finding out facts is hard, but to me it's very rewarding. When I uncover the facts, they turn out to be more spectacular than fiction could ever be. And I'm always on the lookout for what kids in another country are up to, so I can report back to kids here."

Ann grew up roaming the woods of Arkansas. Now she lives in Chicago. She is the author of more than two hundred books for children and young adults on American, European, Asian, and African history and culture. Ann has also written numerous newspaper, magazine, and encyclopedia articles. She holds bachelor's and master's degrees in piano performance. More recently, her performing arts are t'ai chi empty-hand and sword forms. She is an award-winning martial artist and has participated in regional and national tournaments.

Photo Credits